"Every Day Was An Opera

A Libretto By

Maureen Elizabeth Gwilliam

Begun March 2013- 03- 08
Completed June 2014. Published 2014.

<u>"Every Day Was An Opera"</u>

Therefore: Forthwith:

The Control of Any Form of Usage of this Said Work
"Every Day Was An Opera" is Solely that of its Sole Creator Author
Maureen Elizabeth Gwilliam.

Furthermore: <u>No Unauthorised</u> Manufacture, Issuing or Distribution of
Copies of this Libretto in <u>any</u> Format be it Hard Copy, Electronic or
Digital format of this Work " <u>Every Day Was An Opera</u>" will be
Allowed nor Tolerated.
Neither will Distortions Mutilations or Derivatives or Adaptations of
this work be Allowed or Tolerated, without Said Pre Granted
Permission(s).

Thus, Any Performance of this the said Libretto
<u>"Every Day Was An Opera"</u> Hereupon and Hereafter shall and can
only be Performed with Due Granted Permission(s) which will be
subject to Payment(s) of an Agreed Set Fee(s) being Paid in full to
The Author Maureen Elizabeth Gwilliam <u>Prior</u> to the time of any
Performance(s) going ahead.

These said permission(s) can only be granted by The Sole Named
Author myself Maureen Elizabeth Gwilliam
All Such Fiscal Dues and Such Payable Fees are legally due Solely to
Myself The Sole Named Author
Maureen Elizabeth Gwilliam In Perpetuity.

These stipulations I look to and wish to be enforced in perpetuity in
benefit for myself and in future be a transferred benefit for and to my
subsequent willed beneficiaries upon my death.

FURTHERMORE

"EVERY DAY WAS AN OPERA"

All The Music And Song Lyrics and Arrangements Used Throughout This
Libretto
"EVERY DAY WAS AN OPERA"
are Copyrighted to Wendy Guevara

THIS LIBRETTO WAS CREATED
WITH ALL DUE PERMISSIONS GRANTED BY WENDY GUEVARA
TO ME ALONE MAUREEN ELIZABETH GWILLIAM

This Libretto " EVERY DAY WAS AN OPERA"

Is a Fiction based upon my; Maureen Elizabeth Gwilliam (s) Creative interpretation
of the Music and Song lyrics and Arrangements of Wendy Guevara and as such
was inspired by the following Music Performed Written Produced and Arranged
by Wendy Guevara:

The Music and Song Lyrics used within this Libretto were first Produced as
and within Albums Issued by
Wendy Guevara & Guevara Records
ALL RIGHTS RESERVED

The Inspiration to Produce this Libretto / Musical
"EVERY DAY WAS AN OPERA" was inspired by Wendy Guevara's music
contained within
These Two Original Albums:

Diversity Exposé

Originally Performed by Wendy Guevara
Published by and Copyrighted To
Wendy Guevara and Guevara Records 2010 Guevara 001CD

Destiny Dreams Desire

Originally performed by Wendy Guevara
Published by and Copyrighted To
Wendy Guevara and Guevara Records 2013 Guevara 002CD

3

THE LIST OF WENDY GUEVARA'S MUSIC & SONG LYRICS
USED IN ORDER: ARE AS FOLLOWS:

Desire

Wake Up to the Radio

Everyday Is Like an Opera

Sometimes I Feel Like A Motherless Child

But Aren't You A Jamaican?

Live Without Fear

Just Go!

It's All For Love

All You Want From Me

Tick Tock

WENDY GUEVARA
DESTINY DREAMS DESIRE

GUEVARA002CD

It's A Wonderful Day

Before We Met

We'll Fight

Let's Step Back In Time

Setting The Standard

Chained In My Mind

A Home That's All Mine

Someone Out There

On The Rise Again

My Destiny Is Calling

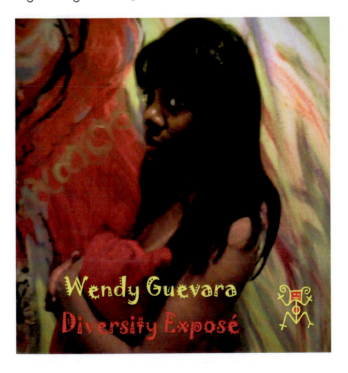

CONTENTS PAGES

END OF PART ONE

Pg. 220

END OF PART TWO

END OF MUSICAL

Pg. 328

<u>NOTE:</u>

<u>Some Characters slip in and out of Trinidadian Dialect according to place and time, and circumstance.</u>

<u>For example whilst in London an English accent is used as much as is possible.</u>

<u>This mainly applies to:</u>

Melanie James

Moira James

Michael James

Grandma

Cherie

Marie James

<u>Other times the speech it can be a mash up.</u>

<u>STEUPS</u>   Trini Speciality
                                Sucking Teeth in Annoyance
                                Can be used as and when required

List of Characters

Melanie James

Beautiful. Begins as a
Young Teenager.
Later in Early Twenties.
Always 'respectably' dressed.
Shy yet strong. Studious.
Serious. Later determined.
Melanie is very much at odds
with her Mother Moira.
Melanie seems to be the only
member of the family who, if
only in small ways; regularly
challenges Moria's dominance.

Moira/Mummy James

Attractive. Striking. Vivacious.
A Matriarch. Late thirties to
Forties. Religious on the surface.
Domineering.
Can be manipulative
Opportunistic. Very well dressed.
Middle Class Trinidadian.
Not an intellectual, but
intelligent and quick to protect
her own interests. She does not
show any love toward Melanie.

Michael/ Daddy James

Intelligent Educated Professional.
Middle Class Trinidadian.
Casual, Smart. He is unaware of
realities of the family's
dynamics. Easy going character.
Michael is slightly older than his
wife.
Reasonable looking.
Thought himself lucky to have
caught such a good-looking wife.
He is under the (Moira's) thumb.
Maybe Spent some years
regretful.
Some how still a little in love with
Moira.. Despite everything.

<u>Grandma (Mummy's Mummy)</u>	Intelligent warm and loving. Grandma is Protective, caring and Wise. Fun – Loving. Trinidadian.
<u>Cherie</u>	Fun loving too. Cherie is Melanie's Pretty Peer. Her best Young Teenage Friend in Trinidad. Later; in her Early Twenties. She is kind and trustworthy.
<u>Marie James</u>	Melanie's Younger Sister. Aged around Ten years at the start. Later; Younger Teenager. Marie is pretty. She resembles her Mother. Marie is very immature for her age. Marie is Moira's favoured daughter. Marie is very much influenced by her Mother. She is obedient and unworldly. Marie is dominated by and kept childlike by Moira.
<u>Partygoers in Trinidad</u>	Various vivacious Young Trinidadians'.
<u>Melanie's Girl - friends in London</u>	
<u>Carrie</u>	British. British Jamaican Father. White English Mother. A bit edgy, somewhat argumentative.
<u>Betsy</u>	British. Two Jamaican Parents. Sometimes the Peacemaker of the group.

<u>Joanie</u>	British. Kind nature. Peacemaker White English Father. Jamaican Mother.
<u>Older & younger School children</u>	Variable bunch.
<u>Miranda Party Guest</u> London	Middle aged white female work-colleague of Moira's in London. Miranda is Racist and hypocritical, opinionated. Believes and thinks of herself as superior.
<u>1st Young Man at Party</u> in London	White male. Obnoxious, Sexist and Racist. Ringleader.
<u>2nd Young Man</u>	Mixed Male. Confused. Trying to be fully accepted as 'one of the boys.' (Only the boys happen to be White.) He is playing down or in denial of his heritage.
<u>3rd Young Man</u>	White Male. Follower of First White Male. Also Obnoxious.
<u>Unknown Offending Male</u> in Melanie's Bedroom	Quiet. Controlling. Menacing, and Violent. Sex Offender. Could be anyone. For the audience to guess on / speculate as who he may be.
<u>Simon</u>	Melanie's Boyfriend / Later Husband. Early Twenties. White Middle Class. English. Educated aware and Loving. But somewhat out of his depth in this situation. Becomes Confused. He is Honest.

<u>Teenagers/ Early Twenties</u>
<u>Mixed gathering in Dance Hall.</u>   London Crowd.

<u>Simon's Friends</u>   White English Males. Early
Twenties. Smart Casuals.
Middle Class. Well behaved.

<u>Random Boy</u>   Dancer + Deep male Voice Singer

<u>Wedding Guests</u>   Mixed ages and Ethnicity's.
Mainly Londoners.

<u>Band</u>   Three to Four guys. Smart.

<u>Band Singer</u>   Black British Female.

<u>DJ (Silent)</u>   At Side of Stage

<u>Simon's Best Man</u>   At side of Marquee (Silent)

<u>God Like Doctor Figure</u>   Older Male. Open To
Interpretation.
Almost a 'Spirit' entity.
But Old Fashioned.
Must wear white Coat.
Distant/Cold / Unaware
Doctor like / God Like Figure.

<u>University Friends London</u>

<u>Jenni</u>   Younger than Mel. Working
Class. Edgy, street - wise.
Small and wiry.
Quick mannerisms.
More sharp than intellectual.
Londoner. Poor. Mixed?
Looks reasonable.
Always in jeans.
Bouncy to cover her feelings of
inadequacy. Jenni admires
Melanie, but is slightly in awe of
her abilities. She is Kind.

<u>Josh</u>	Again, slightly younger than Melanie. But older than Jenni. Clever. White Working class. Not from London. Poor. Always hungry. Thin and wiry too. Josh has Blonde hair with blue eyes. Good looking. He is not aware of it. Josh wears Usual student attire of Jeans and T-Shirt. A bit scruffy. Good heart. Really fancies Mel. This feeling not reciprocated, but Mel likes him. They remain friends.
<u>University Students In Bar</u>	Variable Cosmopolitan crowd.
<u>Two Sound Tech Guys</u>	Young. Dressed In Black. Busy and competent.
<u>Ms Jones Lecturer</u>	Middle Aged White Female. Younger Appearance. Trendy short haircut. Understanding, and aware of her Students' problems. Wanting to help.
<u>Mr Downes Lecturer</u>	Middle Aged White Male. A bit grubby at the Edges. Only around because he wants to be around Ms. Jones. Harmless enough. Slightly clumsy.
<u>Mr Brookes/ MC</u>	Younger than the Lecturers. Mild mannered and helpful. Bespectacled. Untidy. Probably a Ph.D. Student helping out.

Student Crowd	London Crowd. Mixed. Cosmopolitan.
Passers By	Part of Student Crowd.
Bella	Owner of French Farmhouse. Friend who gives advice and an oasis to Mel in her time of need, and a chance to re- group.
	Bella is White, and a decade older than Mel. She is young enough to empathise and old enough to understand with wisdom of experience.
	Bella is Attractive. Dresses very casually in trousers.
Dancers	Interspersed Throughout

Song List In Order of Appearance

PART ONE BEGINS

Scene One

Desire	2x Small Pan **Instrumental** excerpts emanate from the small Steel Pan Band; continues Intermittently.
DESIRE	**Full VOCAL Version** Emanates from the c.d. Player.
DESIRE	Repeat **Full VOCAL Version** From the c.d. Player
DESIRE	Repeat Smaller vocal Girls Melanie & Cherie **Humming along and mimicking**
	Soft Pan beats (As the Girls Melanie & Cherie go to sleep) Small Pan Band Intermittently >

Scene Two

WAKE UP TO THE RADIO	**Full VOCAL Version** emanates from the Radio Melanie & Cherie Sing & Dance along to The Radio

Scene Three

Wake Up To the Radio	**Vocal** Version3/4 From Radio Melanie & Cherie join in again, plus dance a little.
Everyday Is like An Opera	**Instrumental** Version Only. ½ Of Track only. Ends Scene.

Scene Four

Wake Up to The Radio

Melanie **Hums/ Sings** a little snippet along to the Radio

Scene Five

Sometimes I Feel Like A Motherless Child

Small part **Sung/ Hummed** by Melanie & Grandma.
And **Sung** From Off Stage Partial

Scene Six

Everyday Is Like An Opera

Hummed by Melanie x3 in Grandma's Sitting Room

Every Day Is Like An Opera

¾ Lush Strings Quiet **Instrumental**

Scene Seven

SOMETIMES I FEEL LIKE A MOTHERLESS CHILD

Full VOCAL Version

Sung by Melanie whilst kneeling down in Sitting Room of London home

Scene Eight

BUT AREN'T YOU A JAMAICAN?

Full VOCAL Version

Sung by Melanie, backed by Carrie, Betsy & Joanie et al. In Schoolyard. (Along with smaller and older groups of girls.)

17

Scene Nine

Soft Pan Music

<u>Instrumental</u> from c.d. Player
Use parts of Live Without Fear x3

Scene Ten

Soft Beat Pan Music

Muffled soft <u>beat Instrumental</u>
heard from downstairs Party.
Muffled clink of Glasses and
Voices.
Use parts of Live Without Fear.

Scene Eleven

LIVE WITHOUT FEAR

<u>Full VOCAL Version</u>

Full Version. Sung by Melanie in
London Sitting Room morning
after Mummy & Daddy's Party.
The full force of the previous
nights attack upon her affects
her. She cries, and then defiantly
sings this song.
She has been clearing up after the
party. Her parents have left for
work

Scene Twelve

Live Without Fear

<u>Hummed</u> by Melanie.
Partial Vocal " She's a lone and
true survivor">

<u>Scene Thirteen</u>

<u>EVERY DAY IS LIKE AN OPERA</u>

<u>(Full VOCAL Version)</u>

MELANIE SINGS. Whilst
MOIRA/MUMMY remains on
stage.

<u>Scene Fourteen</u>

Just Go!   <u>Instrumental</u>
                                            Disco Version. Sets up the
                                            Dance Hall Scene
                                            (Emanates from Silent D.J.)

<u>IT'S ALL FOR LOVE</u>

<u>Full VOCAL Version</u>

Sung By **Melanie** (Dance Hall
Scene)

It's All For Love   <u>Instrumental</u> Background Beat
                                            Dance Hall Scene
                                            (Emanates from Silent D.J)

<u>ALL YOU WANT FROM ME</u>

<u>Full VOCAL Version</u>

Sung by Melanie Dream Like.
Regarding Simon. Set in Dance
Hall.

Scene Fifteen

TICK TOCK   Full VOCAL Version

                                              Sung by Female Singer
                                              with the Band at Simon &
                                              Mel's Wedding.

IT'S A WONDERFUL DAY

                                              Full VOCAL Version

                                              Sung By Melanie. Set In
                                              Wedding Marquee

BEFORE WE MET

                                              Full VOCAL Version

                                              Sung By Female SINGER
                                              with the Band Set in
                                              Wedding Marquee

END OF PART/ACT ONE

<u>Song List in Order of Appearance</u>

<u>PART/ACT TWO BEGINS</u>

<u>Scene Sixteen</u>

<u>WE'LL FIGHT</u>

<u>Full VOCAL Version</u>

Melanie Sings.
Then Simon joins in.
Set In Simon & Melanie's
Bedroom in their London Flat.

<u>Scene Seventeen</u>

WE'LL FIGHT

<u>Partial VOCAL Reprise</u>

Slow, Sad and soft. (I.e. Voice
then instrumental to fade)
Melanie, then Simon joins in/
<u>into Instrumental</u>/ into fade.

<u>Scene Eighteen</u>

<u>NO MUSIC</u>

<u>Scene Nineteen</u>

<u>JUST GO!</u>

<u>Full VOCAL Version</u>

Melanie Sings In Student Bar.
Partial, dream-like State.
Latter in REAL, now State.

<u>Scene Twenty</u>

Beat From Just Go!

Instrumental Background Beat

<u>LET'S STEP BACK IN TIME</u>

<u>Full VOCAL Version. Full On.</u>

Melanie Sings in Bar Gig.

<u>Let's Step Back In Time</u>	Instrumental Parts / Background Beats

<u>SETTING THE STANDARD</u>

<u>Full VOCAL Version</u>

Melanie Sings in Bar Gig.
Full on.

<u>Scene Twenty- One</u>

Chained in My Mind	<u>Partially Hummed</u> By Melanie (Whilst in Garden in Hammock)

<u>CHAINED IN MY MIND</u>

<u>Full VOCAL Version</u>

Sung by Melanie whilst dreamily walking in Garden.

<u>Scene Twenty- Two</u>

Everyday Is Like An Opera	<u>Reprise VOCAL Snippet</u> "Please allow me to have my say, We could be the best of friends" (In Background)
<u>DESIRE</u>	<u>Partial/Then Full VOCAL Version</u> Heard off stage from Party. (Followed by Big Dance scene in garden.) Emanates from c.d. Player
<u>Scene Twenty- Three</u>	NO MUSIC

Scene Twenty- Four

A HOME THAT'S ALL MINE

Full VOCAL Version

Melanie sings to the Audience.

Scene Twenty- Five

SOMEONE OUT THERE

Melanie Hums to herself whilst playing at Piano.
Later:

Full VOCAL Version

Melanie Sings whilst playing at her Piano.

Scene Twenty- Six

But Aren't You A Jamaican?

Betsy, Carrie & Joanie SNIPPET With small Dance

ON THE RISE AGAIN

Full VOCAL Version

Melanie sings as if in Concert.

MY DESTINY IS CALLING

Full VOCAL Version

Melanie sings as if in Concert.

Everyday WAS Like An Opera

Full VOCAL Version + CHORAL

Melanie et al/ Choral Version.

My Destiny Is Calling

Melanie and Mummy / Moira
Sing together especially on
' My Mamas words return to
me>"

Latterly Sung by The Full
Company as Melanie walks off
stage.

THE END OF THE PLAY / MUSICAL

DANCE LIST PART/ACT ONE

FIRST SET DANCE   SCENE ONE

(Party) Dancing > Interspersed.

Begins with
(Intermittent soft pan music from band)

Mimic dance from Mel & Cherie.

Party goers dance to FULL Vocal Version Song **DESIRE / FULL SET DANCE**

SECOND SET DANCE   SCENE ONE

(Party)

PARTIAL Vocal Song DESIRE.

SOFT PAN
Partial Dances.

THIRD SET DANCE   SCENE TWO

(Girls Bedroom)

Mel & Cherie dance
To FULL Vocal Song Version.
WAKE UP TO THE RADIO/ FULL DANCE

FOURTH SET DANCE   SCENE THREE

(In Kitchen)

Reprise ¾ Vocal Version Song
WAKE UP TO THE RADIO
¾ DANCE by Mel & Cherie

TWIRL   SCENE SIX

                         (In Grandma's Sitting Room)

                         Melanie & Grandma to:
                         EVERY DAY IS LIKE AN OPERA
                         Little Waltz Then, Half – Spin

FIFTH SET DANCE   SCENE EIGHT

                         (Set in Schoolyard)

                         BUT AREN'T YOU A
                         JAMAICAN/FULL DANCE
                         FULL Vocal Version Mel, Carrie, Joanie
                         & Betsy et al.

SIXTH SET DANCE   SCENE FOURTEEN

                         (Dance Hall)

                         Opening with dancing to:
                         Just Go Instrumental Disco Version.

                         Some Impromptu Dancing.

                         IT'S ALL FOR LOVE/ FULL SET
                         DANCE

                         To FULL Vocal Version.
                         Mel, Carrie, Betsy & Joanie
                         Later et al.

                         ALL YOU WANT FROM ME/
                         FULL DANCE

                         To FULL Vocal Version
                         Two Dancers behind Melanie.
                         Smoochy.

SEVENTH SET DANCE   SCENE FIFTEEN

Wedding Guests dance to **TICK TOCK**
(Wedding Marquee)

Twirl by CHERIE before:

IT'S A WONDERFUL DAY Sung By Mel
FULL Vocal Version.

EIGHTH SET DANCE   SCENE FIFTEEN

(Wedding Marquee)

BEFORE WE MET/Sung by Band & Singer

(Wedding; last Dance for Mel & Simon. Later includes With Cherie)

END OF PART/ACT ONE

DANCE LIST PART/ACT TWO

NINTH SET DANCE

SCENE NINETEEN

(Bar Dreamy Sequence)

JUST GO/ Sung By Mel
FULL Vocal Version.

Jenni & Josh Dance,
Plus Students / Dancers
Throughout the Song.
Dream Sequence and in
Real Time / Now.

TENTH SET DANCE

SCENE TWENTY

Student Union Bar /
Dance Hall.
Begins with Students
dancing to background
beat of Just Go!

Set Dance to:
'LET'S STEP BACK IN
TIME. Sung by Mel From
the Stage.

Some of Crowd Sway to
SETTING THE
STANDARD
Sung by Mel from the
stage.

ELEVENTH SET DANCE

SCENE TWENTY- TWO

Set In Bella's Farmhouse &
Garden in France. Party
Scene. Reminiscent of
Trinidad scenario.

Partygoers, Bella & Mel In
and around Garden.

TWELFTH SET DANCE

SCENE TWENTY- SIX

(Theatre Concert Scene)

I'M ON THE RISE AGAIN

Sung by Mel as if in
concert.

MY DESTINY IS
CALLING

Sung by Mel as if in
concert.

Dancers behind Mel
Particularly during
My Destiny Is Calling

Small Dance From Carrie,
Joanie & Betsy whilst
singing But Aren't You A
Jamaican (Snippet)

END of Dance List

<u>CAST LIST IN ORDER OF APPEARANCE</u>

<u>PART/ACT ONE</u>

<u>Scene One</u>

Set in Garden, and Girls Bedroom

MELANIE James	LEADING ROLE
	Scene One
MATRIACH "MUMMY"	Co FIRST ROLE
/ MOIRA James	Scene One
CHERIE	COUSIN / FRIEND
	Scene One
Small (Steel) Pan Band. Young Males	Scene One
1st Young Man at Party	Scene One
2nd Young man at Party	Scene One
<u>Many Party- goers Girls & Boys</u>	Scene One
<u>(Glimpses) of Adults in House</u>	Scene One

<u>Scene Two</u>

<u>Set in Girls Bedroom.</u>

Melanie	Scene Two
Cherie	Scene Two
Moira/ Mummy	Scene Two

Scene Three

Set In Kitchen of James' Family Trinidad Home.

PATRIARCH "DADDY" / MICHAEL James	Co FIRST ROLE Scene Three
MARIE James	YOUNGER SISTER Scene Three
Mummy/ Moira	Scene Three
Melanie	Scene Three
Cherie	Scene Three

Scene Four

Set In Sitting Room James' Family Home in Trinidad.

Melanie	Scene Four
Moira/ Mummy	Scene Four
Daddy/ Michael	Scene Four
English Voice on Radio	Scene Four

Scene Five

Set in Grandma's Old Fashioned Kitchen in her Traditional Trinidadian Home.

GRANDMA	Scene Five
Melanie	Scene Five

Scene Six

Set in Grandma's Cosy Old Fashioned Sitting Room in Her Traditional Trinidadian Home.

Grandma   Scene Six

Melanie   Scene Six

Moira's Voice on Telephone   Scene Six

Scene Seven

Set In James' Family Home in London. Sitting Room.

Melanie   Scene Seven

Mummy / Moira   Scene Seven

Grandma's Soul   Scene Seven

Scene Eight

Set In London Schoolyard.

1st Teenage Girl CARRIE   Scene Eight
(Jamaican Dad White Mum)

2nd Teenage Girl BETSY (Black)   Scene Eight

3rd Teenage Girl JOANIE   Scene Eight
(White Dad, Black Mum)

Melanie James   Scene Eight

Marie James (Younger Sister)   Scene Eight

Younger Crowd of Schoolgirls (Mixed)   Scene Eight

Older Crowd of Schoolgirls (Mixed)   Scene Eight

Scene Nine

Set In James' Family London Home. Sitting Room.

Melanie   Scene Nine

Moira/ Mummy   Scene Nine

Michael/ Daddy   Scene Nine

Miranda   Scene Nine
(Party Guest. White Female
Adult work colleague of Moira's)

First White Young Man. Guest.   Scene Nine

Second Mixed Young Man. Guest.   Scene Nine

Third Young White Man. Guest.   Scene Nine

Various Party Guests   Scene Nine

Scene Ten

Set In Melanie's Bedroom. James' Family Home in London.

Melanie   Scene Ten

Unknown Male   Scene Ten

Scene Eleven

Set In Sitting Room. James' Family Home in London. Next Morning.

Melanie   Scene Eleven

Moira/ Mummy   Scene Eleven

Scene Twelve

Set In Same Sitting Room. Early Evening of same Day.

Melanie	Scene Twelve
Marie	Scene Twelve

Scene Thirteen

Setting: Same Sitting Room. Later That same Evening.

Moira / Mummy	Scene Thirteen
Michael/ Daddy	Scene Thirteen
Melanie	Scene Thirteen
Marie	Scene Thirteen

Scene Fourteen

Setting: Young Persons Dance Hall in London.

Melanie	Scene Fourteen
Carrie	Scene Fourteen
Betsy	Scene Fourteen
Joanie	Scene Fourteen
Boys at Dance Hall	Scene Fourteen
Girls at Dance Hall	Scene Fourteen
Simon (White)	Scene Fourteen
Simons' Friends	Scene Fourteen
Random Boy	Scene Fourteen

Dancers	Scene Fourteen (Dancing Throughout. Just Two Dancers at the END of the Song)
DJ Silent	Scene Fourteen

Scene Fifteen

Setting: Opens in Marquee. Set up in James' Suburban Family Garden. London.

Melanie	Scene Fifteen
Simon	Scene Fifteen
Cherie	Scene Fifteen
Wedding Guests Varied /Ages	Scene Fifteen
Band	Scene Fifteen
Female Singer in the Band	Scene Fifteen
Mummy / Moira	Scene Fifteen
Daddy / Michael	Scene Fifteen
DJ (Silent) in background at side of Stage.	Scene Fifteen

PART/ACT ONE ENDS

<u>CAST LIST IN ORDER OF APPEARANCE</u>

<u>PART/ACT TWO</u>

<u>Setting: Simon & Melanie's Flat London.</u>
<u>In their Bedroom.</u>

<u>Scene Sixteen</u>

Melanie   Scene Sixteen

Simon   Scene Sixteen

<u>Scene Seventeen</u>

<u>Setting Opens on to Empty Stark Darkened Stage.</u>

God Like / Doctor Figure. White on White.   Scene Seventeen

Melanie   Scene seventeen

Simon   Scene Seventeen

<u>Scene Eighteen</u>

<u>Setting: Halls of Residence Campus.</u>
<u>Bed – Sit Room. Single Bed: Desk: Wardrobe and Chair.</u>

Melanie   Scene Eighteen

Jenni & Josh   Scene Eighteen

Simon (Reappears)   Scene Eighteen

Scene Nineteen

Setting: Student Bar. Big Space. / Opens as a Dream like Sequence.

Melanie	Scene Nineteen
Josh & Jenni	Scene Nineteen
Simon	Scene Nineteen
Moira/ Mummy's Voice	Scene Nineteen
Students/ Dancers in Bar	Scene Nineteen

Scene Twenty

Setting: Opens in Same Student Bar. Later that Same Night.

Two Sound / Tech Guys.	Scene Twenty
Lecturer Female Ms Jones	Scene Twenty
Lecturer Male Mr. Downes	Scene Twenty
Mr Brookes /MC /at desk	Scene Twenty
Jenni & Josh	Scene Twenty
Melanie	Scene Twenty
Grandma (In Spirit)	Scene Twenty
Moira/ Mummy's Voice	Scene Twenty
Student Crowd/ Dancers	Scene Twenty
Passers by	Scene Twenty

Scene Twenty- One

Setting: Beautiful Colourful Garden in South of France. HOT DAY.

Bella   *Scene Twenty- One*

Melanie   *Scene Twenty- One*

Scene Twenty- Two

Setting: Rustic Sitting Room in Bella's Farmhouse.

Outside: Fireworks can be heard from the local Fete.

Melanie   *Scene Twenty- Two*

Moira / Mummy (on 'phone)   *Scene Twenty- Two*

Bella   *Scene Twenty- Two*

Party – Goers Varied   *Scene Twenty- Two*

Scene Twenty- Three

Setting: Back In London. Dark Wet Street.
Mel is walking along wearing a coat and carrying a hold all.
Plus two plastic bags.

Setting later turns into Sitting Room of Small run down & drab
London Flat. Home of Jenni & Josh.

Melanie   *Scene Twenty- Three*

Jenni & Josh   *Scene Twenty- Three*

Scene Twenty- Four

Melanie   Scene Twenty- Four

Scene Twenty- Five

Setting: Melanie's own Beautiful Sitting Room.
With Piano.
Many Flowers and Plants.
Some Years Later

Melanie   Scene Twenty- Five

Person on Telephone   Scene Twenty – Five

Moira/ Mummy (on Telephone)   Scene Twenty - Five

Scene Twenty- Six

Setting: As a Theatre.

Melanie   Scene Twenty -Six

Grandma (Visible Spirit)   Scene Twenty- Six

Simon   Scene Twenty- Six

Mummy/ Daddy   Scene Twenty- Six

Cherie   Scene Twenty – Six

Carrie, Betsy & Joanie   Scene Twenty – Six

Marie   Scene Twenty- Six

Bella   Scene Twenty- Six

Et al   Scene Twenty –Six

Three Young Men (In Black hoods)   Scene Twenty - Six

Band 'on Stage'   Scene Twenty- Six

Dancers   Scene Twenty - Six

<u>DIRECTION</u>

All Characters (apart from Melanie) appear as " ghostly " figures.
Some of whom are actually dead; seen and heard as Visible Spirits.

And some are just memories remembered; Seen and heard as Visible
Spirits.

THE END of THE PLAY /MUSICAL

'Everyday Was An Opera'

LIBRETTO

Written

By

M. Elizabeth Gwilliam

<u>PART /ACT ONE BEGINS</u>

SCENE ONE

<u>SETTING:</u>   <u>GARDEN.. SULTRY EVENING IN TRINIDAD.</u>

A Traditional Trinidadian house set in its' own pretty garden.
From a few trees hang lanterns of light, amongst plenty of colourful
flowers. (Such as Ohosonia /Wild Poinsettia)
A scented wafting breeze envelops the gathering.
The James' Family home and garden is, for the evening, the hub of a
celebration of teenage cousins' birthday.

Just a short way from the house a cable lead has been run from the
inside of the house to under a tree where a table houses a c.d. player.
This is the main source of entertainment for the evening's party/fete.
On the other side of the garden is a small <u>**Steel Pan Band,**</u> made up of
mainly young men.

Other tables are laden with food and soft drinks.
Chairs are dotted about; some with smaller tables along side.
In the centre a make shift dance surface of wood has been laid.
A laying down if you like the purpose of the evening's soiree.
To dance and have fun.

The group consists mainly of young teenage boys and girls with
smiling faces, all milling about in anticipation of the excitement to
come: Most are already in the mood... grooving to the band's
traditional pan music. One or two adults can be seen hovering by the
open French windows of the house.

<u>DIRECTION</u> (use part of <u>**DESIRE**</u>)

Everyone seems chilled out and happy.. Even though just a few yards
away the chaperoning adults can still (continuously/ intermittently)
be seen mooching about the interior of the house, watching out from the
windows and doors in a semi – chaperoning manner.

This is a special occasion.. And all are determined to have a good a
time as is possible, despite the 'supervision'!
All is of a gentle chilled manner.
And after all gardens have corners made for secrets!
(Note: Mostly speech is in a <u>**Trinidadian Lilt**</u>.)

STAGE SETTING:

The Opening of Scene One continues in the garden; then it changes focus, to opening onto two young girls watching the proceedings below from a first floor balcony.

They are crouching down looking through the rails of the balcony intently and excitedly upon this garden party scene in Trinidad..

(**Background band pan music** / soft beat.
 Intermittent dancing/noises)

It continues as a very warm evening; and a bright and colourful happy scene.

The two watching young girls are dressed for bed, whilst the partygoers below are in pretty flowered dresses, with the guys in fresh white shirts and their best trousers.
Everyone seems to have overloaded on perfumes and after-shave.
This, coupled with the garden flowery scents, is a heavy mix to be sure.

The Two young watchers seem also to be very happy and carefree.

They are giggling, pretty young things, which, it becomes clear, are meant to be tucked up in bed by now... being deemed to be too young to take part in the merriments to come...

<u>SCENE ONE Beginning:</u>

<u>DIRECTION</u>

Opens with soft Pan beat Instrumental played by the Small Steel <u>Pan Band.</u> Playing (<u>Desire</u>) together with some soft <u>Dancing.</u>

<u>OPENING DIALOGUE</u>

<u>MELANIE</u>

"Oh my God! Everyone looks so pretty and handsome.
It's just not fair; we should be down there too!
I'm tired of being treated like a baby!"

<u>CHERIE</u>

" Keep your voice down! We don't want your Mother up here!
* At least this ways we can watch.. That's if we keep quiet.*
I love it when they beat pan "

<u>MELANIE</u>

"Anyhow; whatever happens they can't stop us from hearing.
I love music. Don't you just love it?
It just takes me away from.."

<u>DIRECTION</u>

Melanie hesitates, and looks sad for a fleeting moment..
Cherie looks to her concerned and puzzled.

<u>CHERIE</u>

<u>DIALOGUE</u>

" Away from what Mel?"

<u>MELANIE</u>

" Oh just stuff.. You know what parents are like.. Always on at you
about something or another. Oh! Look!"

44

<u>DIRECTION</u>

Melanie is keen to change the subject and get back to 'spying' onto the scene below. Melanie stands up somewhat, leaning a little over the balcony for a better view.

<u>DIALOGUE</u>

<u>MELANIE</u>

" Looks as if things are really getting going now
Deh practising for carnaval or what?

Heh! Someone has brought new music!
I wonder what it is?

Oh Cherie, can't you just imagine us down there?
Dancing and all sorts..."

<u>CHERIE</u>

" Can't I just! Just look at them wine! "
(Cherie begins to hug herself and swoon around whilst dancing/wining in her own version)

They all of them making style fuh true!
That cousin of yours sure is handsome you know eh eh!"

<u>DIRECTION</u>

This young teenage party scene continues below in the garden ..
Talking; Laughing, teasing, pushing about in fun.
Some couples are canoodling already in quiet spots that the garden offers up, hiding away from the adult's gaze from the house.
The scene is happiness personified.

Music lilting, pan music wafting through the scented garden...continues (<u>Pan</u> Instrumental part of <u>DESIRE</u>)

Simultaneously the girls above are so excited and trying hard to muffle their giggling anticipation of what they believe will be an uncensored insight into teenage/ young adult life...

As the girls watch the scene below they giggle in a self-conscious way, pointing out various scenes; whilst desperately hoping not to be discovered in their quest. They put their fingers up to their lips occasionally in an attempt to keep one another quiet.

This insight into the next stage of life is unquestionably beyond tempting.

Suddenly a handsome young man comes crashing on to the scene below holding a c.d. in his hand high above his head.
He is waving it excitedly.. Making his way to the c.d. player.

DIALOGUE

1st Young Man

" Heh allyuh! .. Listen up now it's come, it came in dis morning... Just today...
Let's put on some sound now..Let's have some real mix.."

STAGE DIRECTION

He continues to rush over to the c.d. player, and puts the c.d. on. Meanwhile, people begin to groan; though some gather around the player to try to see what the c.d. is that he is so excited about.

DIALOGUE

2nd Young Man

" Eh! Eh! What you doing? I was enjoying the pan... what that you doing man we having a bash?
What is sooo good about this then eh?"

1st Young Man

"Just listen to this man, and tell me it ain't the business...
What a great bandoh dem is"

(The steel pan band has now stopped playing and are also gathered around the c.d player)

The young man places the c.d. onto the player, and the music blasts out>)

<u>DESIRE</u>   <u>First SONG Blasts OUT</u>

<u>STAGE DIRECTION</u>

Slowly at first, people start reacting to the track... then they really get into it. Sexy pretend love play and dancing follows>>

<u>THE FIRST SET DANCE SCENE</u> ensues
<u>(FULL Vocal Song DESIRE emanates from the c.d.Player)</u>

<u>DIRECTION</u>

The whole crowd gets into the music..
Even the <u>(Steel) Pan Band</u> join in with dancing.

The two watching girls on the balcony above mimic the scenes, copying the actions below.

Much preening and interaction between the girls and boys in the garden continues.

However, as the watching girls grow a bit louder in their appreciation and 'secret' involvement, this becomes their downfall.

As the song reaches its climax and ending; a powerful woman's voice enters the fray and the story. She can be heard but not seen as yet.

<u>DIALOGUE</u>

<u>MUMMY /MOIRA</u>

"Melanie, Cherie..
Where are you girls? And what are you all doing?
What's that bacchanal I hear? It's coming from up here I know it is."

<u>DIRECTION</u>

<u>As the music stops:</u>

Below, the young crowd falls about laughing, and hugging, and some even clapping. They disperse:
Some go across to the tables for refreshments.
The band goes back to their instruments. They set up again, and begin to play.

Whilst others mill about by the player, checking out the new music.

2nd Young Man walks over to 1st Young Man.
He places his hand onto the others shoulder.

They all continue talking, whilst the **Steel Pan Band** continues to play their version of **Desire.**

 DIALOGUE

2nd Young Man (to 1st Young Man)

 "Heh man you were right on. It's a real mix!
 We have to play it again you know! Really! Fuh true!
Have a proper jump up!"

DIRECTION

Meanwhile Mummy / Moira is still coming up the stairs.
She can be heard but not seen.

DIALOGUE

MUMMY/MOIRA

"What's going on here?
You girls ain't in your beds?... Where you should be.!.
If I find you where you shouldn't be.. Melanie I'm going to lick you for proper if I find you's gone down into that garden now...
That's no place for children to be..."

STAGE DIRECTION

The girls scurry from the balcony and turn to go back inside to their bedroom.

<u>MUMMY/ MOIRA</u> (Continues:)

"I know I should have sent you someplace else..
You, you young en's can't be trusted, Now where are you?"

<u>DIRECTION</u>

Simultaneously, out in the garden below, the excitement continues.

<u>DIALOGUE</u>

<u>2ⁿᵈ Young Man</u> (Continues)

" Heh Man you is so right .. it ain't half bad..
Come on now,
Play it again"

<u>STAGE/ SET DIRECTION</u>

The 1ˢᵗ Young Man puts the same track on again
<u>**DESIRE SONG**</u> SOARS OUT AGAIN Full Vocal Version

<u>**THE SECOND SETDANCE PIECE ENSUES**</u>

<u>DIRECTION</u>

In the garden, the singing and dancing continues for a while.
<u>**The steel pan band**</u> plays and dances along to the c.d. at first, then the
sounds from the c.d. takes precedence.

The scene/ emphasis moves on into the inside upstairs of the house, and
the track begins to fade somewhat into the background.

<u>**SET (SET CHANGE TO Focus upon Girls BEDROOM)**</u>

Pretty 'girly' bedroom .. containing two single beds..
Dressing table, bedside tables.

A Flowery, yet somewhat still child centric appearance.

<u>DIRECTION</u>

The two girls Melanie & Cherie are then seen in their bedroom.
They are flinging themselves onto and then into their beds.
They giggle with a mixture of excitement and some fear.
They pull the covers over themselves.
All this happens with the mixed softened sounds of the music and of
the admonishments of the Matriarch we have yet to behold in the
background.

MOTHER/ MOIRA

"There'll be no more sleep overs for you young lady...
If I catch you's out of bed"...

DIRECTION

.... The music wafts on softly > > **DESIRE repeating**.

The girls are by now fully under the bed covers, with even their heads
covered up.

The Matriarch MUMMY/ MOIRA appears for the first time:
In the bedroom.

The girls have just managed to get back into their beds before she pops
her head around the door. The music fades to a hum almost.

Now all is concentrated on the bedroom scene.

DIALAOGUE

MUMMY/ MOIRA (Spoken in a harsh voice)

" Don't think I don't know you were on that balcony Melanie!
 You are a bad influence on Cherie you know that?
I know it wasn't you Cherie...

Goodness knows why your Mummy allows you to be around Melanie.

Now go to sleep dear.. it's lucky this bedroom is at the back of the
house. It should be quieter soon enough"

DIRECTION

All this is said in a exaggeratedly insincere softer tone.
Moira starts to tuck Cherie in, whilst glowering at Melanie.

DIALOGUE

MUMMY / MOIRA (directed to Melanie)

"I will deal with you in the morning!...

Now you all get to sleep. The fete will soon be over.
It's only a bit of music and such. Nothing for you to be interested in!
When will you learn to obey Melanie!

You are still a child and you will do as I say!"

STAGE DIRECTION

Mummy / Moira leaves the room, closing the door very firmly behind her.
The girls are silent.
They can still just about hear the music dimly and the party noises off.
They wait awhile to make sure MUMMY/MOIRA has gone.

Mel and Cherie begin to hum (Desire) to themselves quietly with the occasional giggle and whispering to one another.
The music in the garden is just a dim soft beat again from **Small Pan Band.**

DIALOGUE

CHERIE (Whispering)

" We will have good times like that soon won't we Mel?"

MELANIE

" Yes we will, at least you will.
I'm not so sure ....   About me that is...
Is she ever going to let up on me Cherie?"

CHERIE

" Of course she will… she's not too bad is she Mel?
But I guess I'm glad she's not my Mother."

MELANIE

" She's bad enough. You don't know what's she's really like…when…
when no-one's around"

DIRECTION

Mel shakes off the mood. Her voice lightens up.. Not wishing to upset
her friend.

DIALOGUE

MELANIE

" No Cherie, I guess you're right. She's not too bad..
Let's go to sleep.

Night- Night Cherie.

 We had a good time anyhow didn't we?"

CHERIE

" I always have a good time with you Mel.
You're my best est friend in the world..

Night - Night…Mel "

DIRECTION

Melanie turns out the bedside light. The girls begin to fall asleep to the
Soft Pan Beats of Music (**Desire**), which can just about still be heard,
emanating from the garden.

 We again see the girls and boys below dancing softly almost but not
quite smooching. Looking for secret places in the garden.

Scene One Ends

SETTING:
NEXT MORNING in the GIRLS BEDROOM.

DIRECTION

MORNING SOUNDS. Birdsong. Kitchen sounds.

The girls are now awake and immediately begin to discuss the previous evening, how unfair their imposed status and treatment is... missing out on the fun, and being treated as children.
In their minds they are grown and ready to venture out into the world..
Even if it is only into Melanie's own garden.
Melanie is sitting up in her bed.. She is wide-awake.

But Cherie is still under the covers and seems to be still a little asleep.

DIALOGUE

MELANIE

" Morning Cherie...Aren't you awake yet?"

CHERIE (Said whilst stretching)

" Mmmmm..."

MELANIE (Continues)

"Wasn't it so exciting last night?

I just wish we could have been down there in the thick of it!
Dancing and singing!

Cherie how come you aren't awake yet!

Just imagine how lovely that would be.

 If I could, I would wake up everyday singing as loud as I am able to...
Wouldn't that be...?"

CHERIE (Interjects in a sleepy voice and fashion:)

"A miracle! Just imagine what your Mother would be saying!

 And No! I'm not awake! Lest while not properly yet!"

DIRECTION

At this moment Melanie begins to imitate Mummy / Moira..
In Melanie's case very well

DIALOGUE

MELANIE

" I can hear her now, I know exactly what she would be saying!

'Shush up now, what's that catawallin you doing?'
You can't even sing properly you know.' "

CHERIE (Now waking up and joining in with her version of the impression!)

" 'Why you aren't even in the choir at church...!

You think God wants to hear a noise like that?' "

DIRECTION

The girls fall out of bed laughing at their own impressions..
Eventually rolling onto the carpet, ending up in a pile.
They sit on the floor continuing their conversation.

DIALOGUE

MELANIE

"Any how one day..
When I'm all grown and have a Home That's All Mine."

DIRECTION

Mel becomes somewhat distracted and dreamy.
Then she switches back into the now.
Mel stands up and starts to walk around the room.
Cherie remains sitting.

<u>MELANIE</u> (Continues)

" Heh Did you hear Mummy and Daddy last night?
Them talking and laughing and such...
They went on 'till real late. Proper bussing ah lime
SO maybe they'll still be asleep...

Seems everyone had a party last night except us!
Yeah everyone liming..

I know!
Let's have our own party now! Let's put on the radio...
I keep it hidden under the bed.. Grandma gave it to me...

AND she makes sure I always have batteries. SO, It's always working."

<u>DIRECTION</u>

Melanie goes over to the bed; she gets down on her knees and stretches
under the bed, throwing out various shoes and items, until she emerges
triumphantly with the Radio!

At this point Cherie jumps up from the floor in an excited mood!

<u>CHERIE</u>

" Brilliant idea... we can practice our moves!
 We have to be ready for when we do get out there into the world!"

<u>MELANIE</u>

" I knew that the thought of music would wake you up properly!"

Mel turns the Radio on and out comes >

<u>WAKE UP TO THE RADIO</u> Second Song blasts out
Full Vocal Version.

<u>DIRECTION</u>

<u>THIRD SET DANCE SCENE</u> ensues>

Immediately the girls scramble to their feet and begin to sing and dance around the room doing the actions from the song: whilst also attempting to sing into their hairbrushes.. (Grabbed from the dressing table.)

It then dawns on them that they may be in for the same admonishments which came their way the previous night>
They attempt to quieten down as the song comes to an end, Shushing one another in the same fashion as they attempted to the night before.

<u>DIALOGUE</u>

<u>MELANIE</u>

"Oh No!....Shush! I can hear someone coming ...
Oh no not HER again!"

<u>CHERIE</u>

" We had better turn it off!"

<u>DIRECTION</u>

From down the corridor can clearly be heard (before being seen) the same voice and tone that was heard last night..

With that, Cherie grabs the radio, and makes for the bed. But too late.

The girls freeze as the Matriarch Moira enters the girls' bedroom.
She has caught the girls in full flight, as Cherie attempts to hide the radio behind her back.

<u>DIALOGUE</u>

<u>MUMMY/MOIRA</u>

"I don't believe it!

You girls are carrying on from where you's left off last night?
Dancing about and all sort of ting like that!

And on a Sunday morning, when you should all be getting
yourselves prepared for the Church with holy thoughts an all.

You get yourselves into that bathroom and be ready downstairs for
breakfast soon you hear me!

We going out sooner rather than later you know!
I telling you now: and yous' had all better be ready in good time.
We don't need to be late you know!"

DIRECTION

With that Mummy /Moira turns to leave; but she hesitates as
something catches her eye. She turns, and focus's on Cherie.

DIALOGUE

MUMMY / MOIRA

" Now what's that you holding Cherie dear?"

DIRECTIONS

Cherie looks down at her hands suddenly realising the pair have been
caught red handed, as the radio is not fully hidden.

She also realises that because she is not Moira's child, she should be
able to get away with a caution. So she decides to claim:

DIALOGUE

CHERIE

" Oh this little thing.
I was showing it to Mel....anie.

A friend loaned it to me.. we,
We were going to see if we could find a Church service...

You know, get ready, get in the mood for the real thing....
We just love hymns and all, but we didn't seem to be able to find too many ....hymns that is"

" Really!" (Said in an unbelieving voice.)

DIRECTION

Moira too realises she can take this no further, and pulls back somewhat.

She stares at Mel as if she knows there is something more to this, but can't work out what it is exactly.
Defeated for now she turns once again to leave.

DIALOGUE

MUMMY / MOIRA (Said thoughtfully)

" Well, I thought I did hear some kind of music.. coming from here.. But it wasn't no hymn that I recognise; it sounded more like some devil music to me!

Anyway's. That's all well and good.

All I know is, there was some noise coming from this room and it didn't sound Godly to me.

Not Sunday music. Not Gods' music..
Maybe I should check on the station for you?"

(Again Moira looks at the girls intently, but decides to let things go for the time being.
Cherie jumps and steps back holding the radio even closer to her.)

MOIRA (Continues)

"Any how...
We'll leave it for now eh?
I advise yous' girls to get ready quickly now.

As I said I expect you all dressed and smart...and down in the kitchen, very soon for breakfast."

DIRECTIONS

Moira goes closer to the door. Then she turns to Cherie once again.
She speaks to Cherie in a falsely endearing manner.

"That was very generous of your friend Cherie.
I wonder do I know them?"

CHERIE

" Erh no I don't think so.."

MOIRA/MUMMY

" Mm, that seems strange to me.
I know all your family's friends I'm sure..
Oh well, I can always ask your Mummy, can't I?

 Now get on girls..."

DIRECTION

With that Moira closes the door very firmly behind her and makes her way back down the corridor out of sight.. still admonishing the girls from off stage.

MOIRA (Said off stage to herself whilst on her way)

" That Melanie is up to something, I just know it,
 I'll find out the truth of it.
 That Melanie is behind that lie.. I know it"

DIRECTION

After a moment, the girls fall in a heap on the bed laughing nervously.
Melanie lets out an exaggerated gasp!

DIALOGUE

MELANIE

" Phew! Oh my God Cherie we're for it now"

CHERIE

" I know Mel, but I didn't know what else to say or do...

 I just thought that if I said it was mine she would leave us alone.
And she has.. at least for now"

DIRECTION

Cherie looks worried. Mel throws her arms around Cherie..

DIALOGUE

MELANIE

" Don't look so worried, we'll be ok...

Thanks for doing it.

If you hadn't said what you did, I would be in the deepest trouble right
now!

And Grandma, she would have another family row on her hands too...

Look, we'll have to distract her somehow.. We'll think of something..

You never know she might forget, but somehow, I very much doubt it!"

DIRECTION

The girls stay sitting on the bed in a pensive silence.

DIALOGUE

MELANIE

" Cherie,.....
I know one thing we can do for now!

Will you keep it for me?
Just for a while.

I don't think I can keep it here any more.. Not for a few weeks anyhow.
And it'll be good for you.
Help you get up for school on time for a change!

You can wake up to the Radio!"

CHERIE

" Well that's true!

Of course I will...
I'll shove it in my bag right now...
And after church; when I get home, I'll find a good hiding place for it.

Don't worry Mel... No one will find it.
And don't worry; she's sure to find something else to moan over."

DIRECTION

Cherie shoves the Radio into the bottom of her bag.

Melanie sighs and relaxes a little.

MELANIE

" I guess we had better get to the bathroom.....As ordered!"

The girls humour returns, laughing and hugging they tear off set towards the bathroom..

Scene Two Ends

<u>SCENE THREE Begins</u>

<u>SETTING / KITCHEN in The James' Family Home in Trinidad later that morning.</u>

<u>SET DIRECTION</u>

The scene moves to cluttering sounds from the kitchen..
Breakfast making and table-setting is going on.
The table is set for five.

Here Daddy /Michael makes his first appearance.
All are dressed smartly, ready for Church appearance.

Michael is busy at the stove cooking breakfast.
He has on an Apron.

Mummy /Moira is sitting at the Table drinking Juice.
Melanie's younger sister Marie is sitting next to Mummy/Moira.
She is also drinking juice.

The two girls Mel & Cherie walk into the Kitchen.
Cherie is carrying her overnight bag, which she places over in a corner of the room.

Michael turns around to greet them.
He seems very happy and buoyant.

<u>MICHAEL /DADDY</u>

<u>DIALOGUE</u>

" Good Morning young ladies! ..

May I say how smart and lovely you are all looking!
You'll all looking a credit you know! Eh eh

I hope you are both hungry now.
I've been cooking up a storm here..

You sit yourselves down and we can get on with eating this good food up Eh Cherie?"

DIRECTION

Both girls smile at Michael and sit down at the table..
Cherie sits next to Marie and Melanie sits opposite Moria /Mummy.

DIALOGUE

CHERIE (Said with ultra politeness)

" That sounds Lovely.
Thank you Mr James. "

MICHAEL

" My Pleasure my dear!

Now you all do justice to my cooking you hear as today I have cooked
an especially good breakfast for us all.."

MOIRA / MUMMY

" Well Daddy I don't know what you talking of as we always have a
specially good breakfast on a Sunday.

It sets us up to hear a good Sermon and meet up with the Lord with a
smile on our faces.

But Daddy, you seem extra excited about this morning I have to say!"

MICHAEL/DADDY

" Well that's true Mummy... that is true, all true...

BUT! today IS an extra especially good breakfast; BECAUSE it IS an
extra special Sunday.

And do you all want to know why that is?"

DIRECTION

Everyone is now staring hard at Michael in anticipation, and, with just a little trepidation, as Michael has a pan full of food in his hand, and has now begun to wave it about, in a somewhat excited fashion.

DIALOGUE

 MOIRA / MUMMY   (Directed to Michael and said in an almost relaxed and good humour)

" I think you should put that pan down on the table Daddy.
and serve up before you drop it! You so excited or what!"

DIRECTION

All three girls pick up on the lightness in the atmosphere, feeling free to laugh.

Meanwhile, Michael places the pan in the middle of the table as told.

He then pulls himself up to his fullest height.
He takes a deep breath and just blurts out the announcement he has to make... with enthusiasm!

DIALOGUE: MICHAEL

 " You all need to know something!
So it might as well be now.
I have a great new job!

(Everyone looks surprised, but somewhat pleased.
Michael takes another deep breath.
He hesitates and then blurts out the rest of his news.)

MICHAEL

"And it is in London no less!

"We are going back to London!.
 And we are going sooner rather than later."

So, what do you all think of that?"

DIRECTION

There is now a hushed somewhat stunned silence around the table.

Every one seems taken aback.
Even Moira seems surprised by Michael's announcement.

Marie is the first to react:

DIALOGUE

MARIE

"So we doing what?"

 (There is a long pause, whilst everyone looks at one another in surprise, if not shock.)

MARIE (Continues:)

"So what's happening? I don't understand.

Mummy! why is every one so quiet? What does Daddy mean?
We going where?

Is something wrong?"

DIRECTION

Moira is initially as shocked as everyone else.

But, she soon regains her composure and begins to act as if she knew of the decision all along.
Moira stands up and glowers at Michael.

 She pours out more juice into the glasses set out on the table, whether they needed it or not.

Melanie puts her hand over her glass... but to no avail, and in consequence Moira spills some juice onto the table.

Ordinarily this would be cause for comment.. But everyone pretends nothing has happened. (Apart from Marie) who is horrified and scared by the mess.

DIALOGUE

MARIE

"Mummy you spilt.."

DIRECTION

This diversion gives Moira some time to gather her thoughts and to think out her tactics. Moira puts the jug down with a jolt.

Moira ignores the spillage (which is ordinarily unheard of).
Moira begins to answer Marie's question.

DIALOGUE

MOIRA/MUMMY

"Of course not baby... Nothing's wrong at all.

In fact everything is just great.
Such an adventure!

Daddy was just announcing some, I mean the exciting news.
I mean to you girls of course.

I already knew, but kept it to myself as it was for your Daddy to tell you all by himself.

After all it is he who has the new job and all ...

HE WHO MAKES THE DECISIONS AROUND HERE!
Being the man of the house and all.. "

DIRECTION

Moira stares intently toward Michael, all the while she speaks.

Moira can hardly believe the news herself; and can just about contain her own feelings of shock mixed with anger.

Moira sits down with almost a thud back into her chair.

As is her character, she changes tack within a breath, as she contemplates the bragging possibilities down at the club.

Moira is thinking of how the ladies will be green with envy.
<u>She smiles a broad smile.</u>

Meanwhile Marie gets up from the table and rushes over to get some kitchen towel to wipe up the spillage.

There continues to be a silent hiatus around the table.

<u>DIALOGUE</u>

<u>MARIE</u>

" Don't worry Mummy, I will clean it up...
I know how you get upset at mess Mummy...
I'll clean it up.."

<u>DIRECTION</u>

Marie busily cleans up the mess very hastily and nervously, she then takes the cloths away...she deals with them at the sink.

Moira leaves the table in order to walk over to the audience.
The other characters are **set in frozen silent limbo.**

<u>DIALOGUE TO AUDIENCE/SUSPENSION</u>

<u>MOIRA</u>

" Wait a minute...
No one can compete with this news at the club, at Church or anywhere else for that matter..

And London AGAIN! They'll be green with envy. I tell you all..

67

Maybe I shouldn't make a fuss after all...
Mmm

The shopping, the swish restaurants, the lifestyle..
I can send regular updates as to how well we are doing...
It could turn out to be way more exciting than our life here!

I mean top dog here is all good and well.
But London.. Oh to be there again!

The opportunities to impress, to keep getting on; why they are limitless!

And he'll be earning a fortune, (Said whilst looking over to Michael)
Which means I can spend a fortune! Have whatever I WANT!

Whenever I want it!"

DIRECTION

Moira walks back to the scene at the table.
She sits back down in her place at the table.

All characters come back to 'life' again.
In the now.

Moira beams at Michael.

DIALOGUE (Back in the present)

MARIE

" There Mummy; Everything's back as it was"

MOIRA/ MUMMY

" That's fine Marie, good girl.
Now sit down and eat your breakfast like the good girl you are.

(Marie takes her seat back at the table, as Moira begins to preside over events:)

What a wonderful Father you girls have!

Isn't that so Cherie dear... Don't they?

And today is as Mr James said. A Special day.
I would go so far as to say it's A Wonderful Day!"

DIRECTION

Cherie nods and smiles weakly in less than convincing agreement.

Cherie is now staring at Melanie, with a worried look on her face.

Cherie then speaks in a squeaky quiet voice.

She is just managing to hold back her tears.

DIALOGUE

<u>CHERIE</u> (Uttered in a flat tone)

"Yes Mrs James, Mr James is wonderful... the news too.
That's wonderful too.."

DIRECTION

Melanie gets up from her chair in order to hug Cherie.

Michael feels the change in Moira.

Her smile has the effect of relief within him.

There is to be no drama. He is now very buoyed up.
He now has/ feels the confidence to continue.

DIALOGUE

<u>MICHAEL / DADDY</u> (Said to everyone in the room)

" You see what a GREAT decision I have made for this family?
This is the start of big things for us.

My girls can go to University in London as I did..
Just like I always planned.

And you will both have a fine choice of husbands.. much wider than here on the Island..

Oh yes, a finer education AND a broadening of horizons for you both. What more could you all wish for?"

DIRECTION

Michael is becoming even more animated pacing about the kitchen.

Maybe over confidant boosted by Moira's reaction… or should that be non- – reaction?

MICHAEL *continues…*

"And Moira, I mean Mummy here, will put into use again being a fine English lady. In fact you all will!

No more Island talk, no more Trini - English for yous', no more mash up
Proper The Queens English from now on, as it should be, oui!

Yes, we shall all have a great life over there.
You loved it there didn't you Moira? I mean Mummy…
And Me! I can't wait to go back.

Anyhow you girls are English born and bred…
So yous' all are just going home again really.

Just home from home; ducks to water, flap, flap, flap" (He' flaps' and laughs)

DIRECTION

At this point Moira flashes Michael a look that says ENOUGH!

There is pause in the proceedings!
Until Melanie pipes up.

DIALOGUE

<u>MELANIE</u>

"But Daddy I don't want to go back...!

All I can remember about England is it being cold and grey..
And it being so unfriendly...they all seem....
Well, unhappy or something.

I don't know."

(Melanie's voice trails off. She pauses with a sad look on her face.)

<u>MELANIE</u> (Continues:)

"I'm happy here with my frens.. with Cherie; with the warmth...

And Grandma! I don't care about all those things you mentioned!
What's to become of Grandma?

All alone without us?
She needs me............and I need her"

<u>DIRECTION</u>

Now Moira stands up to face Melanie.

Only Marie and Cherie remain sitting.

Marie and Cherie look tentatively up at the other three standing over
them in trepidation:
Wondering how the discussion might escalate.

<u>DIALOGUE</u>

<u>MOIRA/MUMMY</u> (Directed to Melanie. Said in a shrill voice.)

"Now that's enough..!

Why is it always you questioning and making trouble?
What's wrong with you? You trying to cause mess up or what eh?

There's plenty of family here to watch over Grandma, and she is fine
and healthy. There is nothing to worry over she.

71

You exaggerating things as usual.
You should be grateful for this opportunity..

Grateful that Daddy cares so much for us all to do this..
Grateful that he can do this ting for us!

Anyhow............... All this upset in front of Cherie and all

Don't you know Daddy is the man of the house and what he says goes?

Just like the Lord teaches us and says..
Haven't you learned nothing all these Sundays?"

DIRECTIONS

At this remark Cherie almost chokes on her juice which she had decided to sip hoping it might stem the tears a little.

Melanie turns to Mummy /Moira abruptly.
She finds her voice and her courage.

Melanie stands face to face to her Mother, again: finding her courage and her voice.

DIALOGUE

MELANIE

" That's a new one on me. That's the first time ever.. "

(Melanie then turns to face her Father, and asks him outright.)

MELANIE

" Has she made you do this?"

DIRECTION

Michael does not answer at first, but looks down at his feet.
He decides to face the situation full on. For a change.

He speaks quietly, and sincerely. Looking straight into Melanie's eyes

Marie looks on, looking frightened and confused. But silent as usual.

Cherie just looks down at the table.
She is now openly crying very quietly, and also feeling embarrassed
by the turn of events.

<u>DIALOGUE</u>

<u>MICHAEL / DADDY</u>

"Never call your Mother she!   (Said sternly)

And   (Said calmly and softly... even kindly)

No Mel... anie.
This time.

(Michael takes a deep breath.)

This time, this is....
This is for me, as well as you all.

This IS my decision and mine alone.
I got the offer the other day and I have accepted.
This job is what I have always wanted.
Don't you see that child?

This is what I have worked hard towards all my life...
All that studying and all.
All those years..

Isn't that so Moira? I mean Mummy.
(Said to/Looking at Moira)

Really your Mother knew nothing about it..."

<u>DIRECTION</u>

At this statement Moira glares violently at Michael....
Because she had just said to the girls she did know of the move.

73

She does not want to be caught out in a lie..
Michael picks up on Moira's fury:

MICHAEL (Sheepishly continues:)

"What I mean is Mummy of course knew of my intentions,
But maybe not the details... you know what I mean and all...

As I am the man of the house...
Head of the family..
I made the final decision.. And that's all there is to it.
We going and that's that. Final fuh true!"

DIRECTION

Michael's voice tails off; and he decides now is the time to wander off
back to the stove and begins to tinker with a pan, which he does in a
relieved but slightly nervous manner.

DIALOGUE

MOIRA/MUMMY

" Yes Daddy, that's just how it was,
And I am so proud of you"

DIRECTION

Michael turns around to look at Moira in shock, and relief.
A slightly embarrassed smile comes over his face..

He continues, thrown off track for a moment by Moira's
embellishment. He is however, flattered too by Moira's support.

DIALOGUE

MICHAEL

" Yes, well, As I was saying. And...
Well, You'll see Melanie.
And you too Marie..   (Said whilst waving a wooden spoon about)

It will be for the best for everyone..

I want you all to be happy.
I want you all to be successful..

I want to be successful!

And I know when we go back you will all get along better than you do
here.. I just know it.

We will all be happier.. A happy English family.
I just know it.

So.. In the end it will work out for the best. I just know it will."

DIRECTIONS

Melanie sits back down, slightly shocked at her Fathers' tone, and at
the fact he has for once stood up to Mummy/Moira.

Mel realises that the situation is now a fait accompli.
There is nothing to be done but accept it.

Cherie bursts into tears, forgetting about hiding her feelings.
Marie continues to look lost.

Melanie stares into space.
Moira remains standing. Moira has the last word.

Moira speaks up.

DIALOGUE

MOIRA / MUMMY

" Well after all that excitement girls, nothing alters the fact we all
should be getting ready and on out to Church...

It looks like we need to speak with the Lord even more so than ever to
seek out guidance, to do the right thing and get ourselves ready for
England..
You too Cherie.

Even though you staying here on the Island... you need to pray for guidance too, in your life.
We all of us always need The Lords' help to do the right thing and all, wherever we are in dis world and we all his children eh."

CHERIE

(Still sobbing a little and speaking quietly)

"Yes Mrs James... I suppose so".

DIRECTIONS

The two older girls' exchange glances.
Michael walks across to the table and places the pan in the middle of the table. He begins to serve up the rest of the breakfast to the women.

Michael then takes up his newspaper from the table and takes it across to a sitting chair placed in the corner of the room.
He begins to read it.. Or pretends to? (Maybe as a diversionary tactic.)

Moira sits back down at the table and stares ahead.

Marie begins to hug Mummy/Moira (who allows the hug for a short time then pushes her away impatiently)

The others slowly begin to sip juice, and play around with the food on their plates, also taking some from the pan left in the middle of the table.

There is some vague attempt to eat the special breakfast.
But no one seems to have their usual appetites.

Michael gets up from his chair to go back to the table and his breakfast and begins to toy with his food too.
All are silent.

Eventually Moira / Mummy is the first to leave the table and the room, followed quickly by Marie; who dashes after her from the table; as usual following in Moira's wake.

Then Michael gets up to leave.
He turns to Melanie, and speaks once again...quite kindly and softly.

<u>DIALOGUE</u>

<u>DADDY/ MICHAEL</u>

" It will be good for us Mel. You'll see.. as for Gran,
Well she not too old you know.. to come over to visit us sometimes...

(He looks to Cherie)

Cherie, you never know when you a full-grown lady you might come
out to see us too.. And meanwhile there are always letters and the
' phone eh?"

With that Michael too leaves the room.

Now only the two girls- friends are left alone to absorb the news.. the
bombshell.

Pensively they stare out into space in silence.

Mel is the first to break the silence..

<u>DIALOGUE</u>

<u>MELANIE</u>

"Looks like you'll be keeping that Radio for a long time now Cherie
Eh?"

<u>DIRECTIONS</u>

They both laugh gently.
The girls get up and start to clear the table..

<u>DIALOGUE</u>

<u>CHERIE</u>

" Damn it Mel. Let's cheer ourselves up!

77

Let's put on the Radio! We may as well now eh?

After all it really is my radio now, so _She_ can't object to it any more..
And I will tell my Mum a friend gave it to me... which is now true.

They'll never work it all out.. and by the time they do you'll all be
gone! So, I guess it all really doesn't matter too much now eh?"

DIRECTIONS

Cherie goes across to her bag and reaches deep inside it.
She brings out the radio...

CHERIE

"Gosh Mel you did say you wanted something to distract her!
But I never dreamt it would be this big!"

MELANIE (Laughing as she sees the irony, then a bit sad)

" All true Cherie..

But I think this is taking things a bit too far eh!
I can hardly believe what just happened"

CHERIE

"I know. Me neither.

I will miss you so much.
But I'll have this to remember you by eh?
(Said whilst waving the little Radio)

I'll treasure it for you .. Your Gran getting it for you and all..

DIRECTION

Cherie clasp's the little radio to her heart

"I guess nothing is ever going to be the same again eh Mel?"

MELANIE

" I guess not Cherie...

But we have so much more to remember one another by Cherie..
So many memories...

You know you are my real sister, don't you?"

CHERIE

" I know... You too!

(Then Perking Up)

Come on let's go mad and put it on!"

DIRECTION

With that Cherie pops the radio onto the breakfast table, and turns it
FULL on.
It blasts out >

WAKE UP TO THE RADIO..   (³/₄ of the song)

DIALOGUE

BOTH MEL & CHERIE (Excitedly)

"Wow it was meant to be! It's **Wake up To The Radio** again!"

DIRECTIONS

The girls begin to Laugh whilst **Singing and Dancing** around the
kitchen table with and to the music.
They continue dancing around to the track.

Moira / Mummy **returns** to the kitchen, in a whirlwind.

DIALOGUE

MUMMY/ MOIRA

" I see you are enjoying your Radio again Cherie! There's no end to it!

And, You just don't seem to be able to find that Godly station you were looking for before at all; fuh true!

I would give up if I were you!...(Said sternly)

Those things can be tricky to find eh Cherie?"

DIRECTION

The girls have been stopped in their tracks. Cherie turns the music off.

CHERIE

" True Mrs James.. very true . It really is hard to find it."

MUMMY/ MOIRA

" Yes, the truth is also hard to find sometimes too Cherie...

(There is an awkward silence....
Moira is staring directly at Melanie.)

However, it sure does have a habit of turning up when you least ways expect it to...
The truth will out! Isn't that what they say Melanie?

Isn't that right Melanie?

I mean you know that much about me Melanie.... Don't you?
I always search out the truth.. I never give up. Do I?"

DIRECTION

The girls are almost standing to attention now....
Whilst shaking their heads.

Cherie is now holding the little Radio behind her back in vain: as if not seeing it might deflect Moira's attention from the whole situation.

MOIRA /MUMMY (Continues:)

"Anyhow girls..."

DIRECTION

Moira pauses to think. She now turns her attention back to Cherie:

MOIRA/ MUMMY (Continues brightly)

" Your Daddy will be here soon Cherie, and we'll all go to Church together.. Like the good sociable Christians we are..

And you can show your Radio you holding behind your back to your Daddy unless of course he has seen it already.. As I have...

But what am I thinking of eh Melanie?

I expect he has seen it plenty of times!
So, you can look for that station with him later
When you got more time eh?

I sure he will be able to find it easy, fuh true. Men good with such tings.
So's you'd best both go get ready now, we all going soon.
I don't know why I have to keep telling you such"

DIRECTION

Moira now changes tack.
Her voice becomes softer and even happy in tone:

She begins to relish the anticipation of giving out her big news to all and sundry:

Moira wafts around the kitchen dreamily:

DIALOGUE.MOIRA/ MUMMY

"It will be so good to share our news with everyone; won't it girls?
Everyone will be in Church today fuh sure!

Why, your Mammy already been at Church for hours doing the flowers and such like. She'll expect you to look your best Cherie, so don't you go letting us parents down now.

You make yourself tidy, good and respectable now.
So run along and get your coat and such.."

DIRECTION

Cherie stars to scurry off making sure she has the radio tightly held to her. She turns to look at Melanie.

DIALOGUE

CHERIE

"Mel…"

DIRECTION

MUMMY/ MOIRA looks sternly at Cherie.
The girls remain standing very still, and scared.

DIALOGUE

CHERIE

"Sorry Mrs James, I meant Melanie, I forgot, I mean Melanie,
Is Melanie coming with us, in our car?"

MUMMY / MOIRA

"Of course. She always do. Now off you go now.
She'll be along later.
Shoo else you'll be late, we'll all be late,
I tired of telling you all such, what with all the excitement and all.

Here don't forget your bag Cherie.
You'll need it to put that precious radio in!
You don't want to be losing things now do you?"

(Moira picks up Cherie's bag from the corner of the room and waves it towards her..
Cherie takes it in her hand.)

MOIRA /MUMMY

"Mr James will be fed up waiting. He standing about the car already
you know..
Men is always ready fast....
They get impatient waiting around and such like..
They not like us having to make ourselves beautiful and all kinds of
tings like that..
For The Lords House.. that is. Respectable ....and such
For to enter The Lords House. Now get along child"

DIRECTION

Moira seems distracted and serious...
Maybe dreaming of her perceived triumph to come when she announces
her news to all.

Cherie leaves with a quizzical look on her face turning once again to
Melanie. She seems worried, and scurries off, with her bag and radio in
tow, in a fluster.

Melanie looks sad as if she knows what is about to come.

Only when Moira is sure Cherie is out of the way does she begin to
speak.

Moira looks around the kitchen. A mist of dislike comes over her.
Her voice is hard. Very hard.

DIALOGUE

MUMMY / MOIRA

" Melanie.
You not going to spoil this for me you know!

(Moira looks around. Melanie has been and is now standing to almost
attention. Mel looks frightened.)

This place is a mess….
Daddy always was a messy cook and all

I've decided you can stay home today as a punishment!

I know all that noise and disobedience has come from you..
You are a bad influence on Cherie you know that don't you eh?

God don't want you in His House that way..
You stay here and get everywhere cleared up...
We will be coming back with your Tanties and such...
So... Get everywhere tidied up
And get something prepared, vegetables and such ready for our
return... no slouching now"

DIRECTION

There are Noises off of getting ready, of finding coats, hats and a general melee.

Moira walks over to get close to Melanie.

Moira squeezes Melanie's arm very tightly, viciously digging her nails into Mel's arm until Melanie lets out a muted squeal.

DIALOGUE (Hissed / said in a low mean voice/ tone)

MUMMY/ MOIRA

" Don't think you are getting away with this, just because we are going away.
I know you are behind all this radio thing. I'll get to the bottom of it ..
you won't lie to me and get away with it..

Now get this kitchen cleaned up. AND remember God sees whatever you do or don't do! And he will tell me all I need to know.

I am your Mother AND don't you forget it. You will obey me! Always!"

DIRECTION

84

Voices off: sounds of car engines..

<u>DIALOGUE</u>

<u>DADDY/ MICHAEL</u> (Calls out, from outside:)

" Cherie's Daddy here!
Aren't you four lovely ladies ready yet?
How long you all gonna take now eh?"

<u>MUMMY/ MOIRA</u> (Delivered in an exaggeratedly light – hearted
voice, whilst still holding on to Melanie's arm)

"We all coming Daddy…
Just a few lady like adjustments to be doing..
We won't be long time now""

<u>DIRECTION</u>

Mummy / Moira turns her face into Melanie's face. She is still
holding fast.

<u>MOIRA</u> (continues to call back in reply)

"Melanie not feeling too well Daddy you know.

 So, I said she could stay home and rest up, after all de tan-ta-na and
such ting like dat.

Too much excitement I think, what with the fete last night and all the
news this morning and all kinds of tings like that."

<u>MOIRA</u> Continues: (Said nastily. As an aside to Melanie only.)

"You shouldn't even be coming to London, it all wasted on someone
like you.
All those pretty clothes and all..

You should stay on the Island, where you belong..
So I'll make sure you do eh?
At last we agree on something eh Melanie?

We bonding at last… all that Mother and Daughter love shining through eh?"

DADDY (Voice heard. Calling from the car)

" Oh, that's a pity she seemed ok a minute ago..
Heh you rest up for all of us eh Mel…anie. We see you later eh?"

MELANIE (Calling through her pain)

" Yes Daddy I will"…

DIALOGUE Cont:

MOIRA/ MUMMY (To Melanie. Digging her nails into her arm even more.)

"Now you go kneel in that corner, you hear, and face the wall.
You know what to do don't you Melanie?"

DIRECTION

Melanie walks across to a corner of the room….Her head bowed.

It is as if she has placed herself there hundreds of times before.
She is well rehearsed.

Melanie seems resigned to her fate. She kneels down to face the wall.

MOIRA /MUMMY

" Put your hands behind your back properly!

 Now you stay there 'til eleven now…

You didn't think I was letting you get away with that sort of thing did you now?

And don't you go bothering your Daddy about all of this..
He's a Man, and Men got better things to think about than silly young girls who disobey.

That's my job to make his life easy at home..
And all you do is disrupt things for him..

And then make all this work for me.

Now I got to hurry and get my hat on..
All the ladies will be looking to me to set a good example, and you is
causing me all this time- wasting trouble with your idiocity."

DIRECTION

Moira leaves the room, then comes back with her Sunday best hat.

MOIRA (Continues to berate Melanie whilst putting her hat on.)

"No body knows what I have to put up with with you...and I'm going to
keep it that way.

You hear me now?
Just you and our Maker knows what you really are Melanie."

MELANIE

" But Mummy you just said I was to clear up, and get the vegetables
ready,....how will I know what time it is? And when to get up!

I can't see the clock from here, and I don't have no watch.

I can't do both tings Mummy? "

DIRECTION

N.B. When Melanie (and Moira) are upset their Trinidadian accent
strengthens.... Conversely also when happy.

DIALOGUE

MOIRA/MUMMY

" Hush up now you stupid girl, people will hear your fuss and
nonsense, you a real stupidee.
(STEUPS a Trini Sound of sucking teeth in annoyance)

You will hear the clock strike eleven, and that's when you know to get up stupid...
And don't say tings.. it is things (said in precise English)
Say tings properly..

Like your Daddy say, there'll be No more Island talk, no more mash up in dis family, fuh true."

MELANIE

" But mummy you say tings sometimes, I mean when you forget that is"

DIRECTION

At this statement Melanie cowers a little, feeling she has gone too far and made the situation worse for herself.

Moira/ Mummy is putting her hat straight and fussing with her hair and attire. She is now checking herself in a mirror.

At this point Moira swings around in a rage!

MOIRA

"Such a LIE!
You don't go blaming me...

It's that Gran of yours' that can't speak English properly..
She ole and hangs on to the ole ways and such things like that......

Now look what you done, you done make me vexed bad, all over again all over some new thing..   And my hat not straight and all.

I swear to the Lord you not just ugly but stupid with it...
At least the Lord gave me one pretty child and she has more sense than you've ever had, and she so young!

Now don't you go thinking you can get up just as soon as we leave now! 'Cos God is looking down at you, and He know all you do!

And He know you not in his House where you should be on a day like this..

So He KNOW ALL what is a going on, He know where you are and why,
And He ain't pleased! I tell you now He ain't pleased.

We all have our cross to bear and The Lord knows you is mine..."

MELANIE

" But Mummy it is you who tell me not to go to God's House, it's you who tell me to stay away..."

MUMMY / MOIRA

"I swear to my Lord you ain't right, you one of them damaged children one of them detracts..
Now you listen out for the eleven chimes. I know you can count to eleven, even a baby can do that! Even you not that stupid and all.

Then get up, and get on.
You'll have plenty of time to do a few vegetables and clear up."

MELANIE

"But Mummy, I want to go with Cherie, I want to go...
I want to be with her.. We going soon and I will miss her so"

MUMMY/MOIRA

'We?
We going!

Who is we?
Don't you understand nothing I say? Nothing?
I tell you, you staying here if I can help it!

Don't you know to respect your Mummy and your Daddy?

That we is always right, that we walk in the way of The Lord?

Don't you know you must obey what we is saying to you?"

DIRECTION

Moira's voice is now increasingly vicious.. But still she is managing to keep it low, so as not to be heard by the others.
Moira drags Melanie nearer (almost into) the wall.
Moira pushes Melanie down harder onto her knees.

DIALOGUE
MOIRA/MUMMY

"Now kneel down properly and face that WALL! As I tell you.

And do as I say, I know what God wants from you.
He want you to think on what you have been doing and saying.
He wants you to REPENT....
And remember Melanie!
These walls have ears a coming out of them and so I'll know what you do and what you say.

You are bad girl and you a bad influence on Cherie.
Cherie is a good girl when she not near you...."

DIRECTION

Moira now directs her words to the sky..
To Her God.
Moira continues:

MOIRA/ MUMMY

"My Lord I have to keep her away from my Little Angel....
My sweet innocent little Marie. You play with dog you must get fleas!

God told me the right name to bless my darling Marie with.
I know THAT now, I know that."

DIRECTION

With that Moira/ Mummy shoves Melanie by the back of her head again and there is a thud heard as Melanie's head hits the wall.

Melanie tears up in her heart but no tears come out.
As Moira leaves the room Melanie turns to watch her Mother go.
Melanie stares with a look of hatred...

This feeling sets hardened in her from then on.
As Moira leaves the room she is calling out:

DIALOGUE

MOIRA / MUMMY

" Aye as I said Daddy, Melanie's feeling really unwell now.

There is no doubt she will have to miss Church!
I know I'm too soft on that girl but I'm letting her rest in her room' till
we get back... "

DADDY/ MICHAEL

"But I don't understand she alright a few minutes ago... If she feeling
so much worse maybe I should I come and have a look at her!"

MOIRA / MUMMY

" Now don't you worry so about her, you leave her to me, you got more
important things to do.

You a Man of the World now. You always was.

Melanie will be fine, it's just lady things and all that sort of thing
like that.
Not for you to talk about..

Anyhow we'll be late at this rate.. And I don't want so today of all
days! Let's go!"

DIRECTION

With that Moira swoops out of the house to the driveway and the
waiting car.
Her voice can be heard carrying on>

"I know I'm too soft with that girl.
What can I say?
It's just a Mother's love...

It will just have to be the three of us...with Cherie and her Daddy of
course "

<u>DADDY/MICHAEL</u> (Sounding bemused, shaking his head)

" Well I expect you do right if she feels ill and all like that
You know what to do and all with such things........."

<u>DIRECTION</u>

Car doors slam, and the engines roar off.

Cut to Melanie kneeling with her head bowed to the wall in one corner
of the Kitchen to the ticking of the clock.
Then:

<u>Scene Three Ends With</u>

<u>INSRUMENTAL MUSIC ONLY</u> version of ½ of Track
(like a Taster)

<u>EVERY DAY IS LIKE AN OPERA</u>

<u>SCENE FOUR BEGINS</u>

<u>SETTING</u>

Opens up in a comfortable sitting room in the James' family home in Trinidad.
The family are preparing to move out to go to London again.
This is a typical scene of half-filled boxes strewn across the floor and of slight chaos.

<u>DIRECTION</u>

Moira is sitting in her armchair.
Melanie is kneeling on the floor at Moira's feet.

They are surrounded by paper and boxes of differing sizes.

They are busy wrapping up various items, such as Ornaments and Trophy's.
At first they are not speaking.
Now and then something is placed into a box.

<u>DIALOGUE</u>

<u>MELANIE</u>

"Mummy I'm going to miss Grandma so much and Cherie.
 They would be so sad to lose me.
And then there is Missy; she's such a lovely cat.

And Mummy, I can't remember too much about London.
What I do remember is that it's so cold and grey all the while.
And the people! They not too friendly towards us…"

<u>MUMMY /MOIRA</u>

"Child what **<u>are</u>** you talking about?
That the Mother Country you talking about!
Mind your manners!

Anyhow, <u>you</u> won't be missing anyone,
You staying here just like you did when you was young…

93

You staying here with Grandma 'till we get set up properly again..
I can't be doing with you around when I'll have so much to do, what
with Marie to take care of and a new home to settle in;
And all sorts of tings like that....

No.
I don't want you around, not with the way you always causing
trouble for me and your Daddy...it too much for me to handle and all..

Having you over there will just make tings wus..."

MELANIE

" Really Fuh sure?
It's all settled so?"

DIRECTION

Melanie sits up and speaks excitedly.
This seems to her to be great news!
Melanie stops wrapping at this to sit up even more.

MELANIE

"Oh!, I thought we were all going,

So, will Grandma be looking after Marie too?"

MUMMY/MOIRA

"What on earth are you thinking of?
I just told you Marie coming with her Mummy and Daddy!

Marie too young to be away from her Mummy!

Why!
Such a thought, you old enough to be with Grandma on your own now.
And it's you who will be doing the caring.
It's about time you act your age.....and did something of use
My; when I was your age"...

DIRECTION

Moira pauses reminiscing in her head?
She also catches her breath, sighs then continues:

MOIRA/MUMMY

"So, you can help take care of Gran for a while.

You the first born..
It is your duty to stay over here awhile and care for her in her old age..
Don't you know nothing? How so?
Didn't I teach you such?"

DIRECTION

Moira shakes her head..

MOIRA/ MUMMY

" All them years of schooling in Sunday School and such..
And you still don't know your duties to your family ..

And any ways, you probably be married soon enough, and all that, so
it would be a waste of good money taking you over there.

So that's been decided now, and anyhow isn't that what you wanted?"

MELANIE

"It is... For once it looks like I am to get what I want!
Grandma and I will be so contented.."

DIRECTION

Moira and Melanie recommence wrapping the ornaments up.
They go back to their tense silence.
Eventually Melanie speaks up:

MELANIE

"You know Mummy when you left me with Grandma before,

I was teeny, much younger than Marie is now.
She could stay too; if it make things even easier for you and Daddy I mean"

DIRECTION

Melanie's voice rises in fear; she and her Mother exchange harsh glances ..
Melanie turns in suspension :

DIALOGUE TO THE AUDIENCE/SUSPENSION

MELANIE

" All I want is to get Marie away from those two..
Especially HER...   (Melanie nods towards Moira)

As things are going Marie will grow up to be like Mummy if she ends up alone with her now..
If only she could be with Grandma and Me..
And Cherie..
I would have my Sister back..

She's so young and impressionable.
She really thinks Mummy's word is God's word.
We could all be so happy if Marie stayed with us.
She would have a chance of learning to think a bit for herself!

I don't need those things Mummy needs.
She's right.
Without me around she can lead that fancy life she is dreaming of.
And Marie could grow up half way 'normal' if she stays with us..
Not be mean like HER!

But somehow I know that's just a pipe dream.."

DIRECTION: Melanie continues to speak to Moira /Mummy

DIALOGUE. Back into 'Real Time'

MELANIE

"Any how I love Grandma so much, I'm glad if I stay....
I'll be here with Cherie and all..

Mummy, just think how much easier it would be for you if Marie
stayed too..
I mean for work and going out and all things like that.

We would all look after her, she doesn't need to go to London."

DIRECTION

Moira stops what she is doing abruptly in order to peer at Melanie.
Melanie continues very nervously.
Her voice begins to tremble..

MELANIE (Continues)

"What I mean is... not just now"

DIRECTIONS

Moira calmly puts down the wrapping paper she was holding.
She leans across and calmly, carefully and deliberately slaps Melanie
hard across the face.

Moira sits back in her chair in silence and smirks in satisfaction.

Melanie drops the paper she was holding in order to hold her face.

DIALOGUE

MUMMY/MOIRA (Eventually: Said in a shrill voice)

" Never tell me what to do with MY Daughter EVER again.
What do you know about what Marie needs or doesn't need?"

DIRECTION

Moira gets up from her chair.
She begins to display her airs and graces to Melanie.

<u>MOIRA/ MUMMY</u> (Continues)

" Marie is MY Daughter.
I know what is best for her, and her future!
And what's more she will do as I say and please.!
As you will!

Do you really think I want Marie to stay here with you and some feeble
ole woman that is soft hearted and soft headed!

Not to mention Un - Godly?

She will let you all do whatever you like to do...
No discipline or nothing!

And my little angel will end up speaking the Lingo, like some low
class Trini.
Be an Islander fuh true! Even end up with some ragamuffin!

What idiocy is this? You mad fuh true!.
It too late for you.. You been here with that ole woman too long..
But my Marie... why it's different for her"

<u>DIRECTION</u>

Moira begins to strut about...venting her rage.

<u>MOIRA/MUMMY</u>

"You soooo right that I want you to stay here with your Grandma.

"You'd be out of place in London, with all those fancy shops and
tings...you better off here, helping out and all such things like that..
You an embarrassment!

Poor Marie having a Sister like you..
You should be someone for her to look up to
Not someone who looks like.. Well I not saying...
And acts like it too sometimes.

You would never blend in over there..
Whereas Marie she got possibilities...big possibilities!

A real chance to marry well and all kinds of ting like that..
She sooo fair and she is sooo pretty..."

DIRECTION

Moira's voice tails off.
Moira bends down and cups Melanie's face in her hands. Moira stares
intently into Melanie's eyes, and face. Melanie stares back.
Mummy/ Moira throws Melanie's head to one side as if she is literally
throwing her away.

Moira straightens up, and continues to strut about the room.
Melanie stays bent over, her head down.

After a while Moira continues her monologue:

MOIRA/ MUMMY

"Don't you know Daddy's job will mean we have to meet lots of fancy
people?

And you, well you just not cut out for that sort of ting.
Whereas, well we can't all be, well, at ease with such folk and all sort of
ting like that. Marie young enough to learn how to mix well and proper
fuh true.

You should be thankful to me... Be grateful. I saving you from
humiliation and such like. As your Mother, I saving you from all dat.

I'm giving you what you want, and I saving you from torment fuh
sure"

DIRECTION

Moira continues to walk around the room, as if practising for the
future in London.
Imagining how she herself will ' blend in'.

Moira finally settles upon the audience.
Melanie remains frozen in her fear.

DIALOGUE TO THE AUDIENCE/SUSPENSION

MUMMY/MOIRA

" Oh the Memories, the beau's, the opportunities,
The opportunities missed!

Never again will I pass up on dem fuh sure!
This time I will take all my chances with both hands!

This Melanie is why I am stuck in this marriage yuh know!
She too like her Father for my comfort you know.

Full of stupid ideas and such.

While Marie,
Oh that Marie she has such potential.. like me.
We two peas in a pod!
What is that saying...
You all English out there so you know what I am talking about eh?

(Said almost as a challenge to the audience to remember it for her)

You know the one about apples not falling down far from the tree!
De fruit don't fall far from de tree eh eh!

Well that is me and My Marie!
She going to get herself a fine pairing up.. make no mistake..

I'll make sure of that! I can tell you!
Not like me eh?

I say! (Said in Mock English Accent)
Why your sayings all about fruit and vegetables eh eh?

Any how ...
Marie won't be needing all that academic stuff Michael always going
on about.

She's a girl.
A proper prim and proper girl.

With all the attributes needed for such. I right eh?"

DIRECTION

Moira makes an old fashioned outline of the female form..

MUMMY/MOIRA

"She attractive fuh sure already!

(Pensive pause)

She learning piano too you know?
And she good at needlework and such.
Just like in those old books of yours.

She going to be a Lady!. She'll read it too..
Fuh true.

A Fine English Lady..
Yes...just like in the magazines and those fancy old stories..

She being brought up properly to understand the things that
important in life.

Like being a lady...
And going to Church..

And making a fine marriage.
Having babies...not too many mind!
And nice babies, I mean."

DIRECTION

At this point Moira looks as if she is cradling a baby..

"I know she young... but she is shaping up well
And she will get everything she needs to make her so right.

And later when she grows up.
Ahhhhh

Just like I should have had. Then I would have married ...
Well never mind all that now eh?

He my husband and that's that.
He tries hard mind you, he tries.

But some things you can't change eh?

And me?

You all thinking about me? Eh?
Ah Well. I need to make the best of it.
And the best of it is to Live **The** Life in London..

What am I saying? You don't need me to tell you all eh?
Looking around I can see you all knows about that for sure;
Living the high life you all eh?

Plenty of meat on all of you eh eh?
(Moira points outwards to the audience)

You got size? No skin and bone eh?

Sooo, While he making it... I'll be spending it.. "

DIRECTION

At this Moira walks about as if she is in a grand shop..
Looking at clothes, pretending to try them on..
Then paying for them..
Carrying a fancy bag..

" Yes, That'll be me
Just like those fancy women do.

(Another little pensive thought..)

My cousins are over in America and such like
They got plenty money too!
But I don't mind New York; it has good shops too eh?
But then so does London..
And he got the job there and all..
And I liked it good enough before.. what with The Queen and all that..
The Mother Country fuh true eh?
You all want us bad eh!

To build up and all kinds of ting like that..
And he clever you know.. That Michael.
I'll say that for him..
Not much of a looker, but he make good money and all.
He generous too... not mean like some men can be eh?

And in the end you never know I might just get those light-skinned grands..

They say it happens ...Creole and such like.

In the mix and all.
That's one thing I will never get from her "

DIRECTION

Moira turns to glower with hatred at Melanie.
Her voice gets even harder.

" I mean just look at her.
She DARK and that nose and all
Ugh...   (Said with a shudder)

 I know I a bit dark and all...
But Melanie she ...   (Said with another shudder)

Now Marie..
She
Thank the LORD is not like Melanie's Father.
Don't you all think she Pretty?

She take after...   (Moira suddenly stops. Pulling herself up)

Well never mind who she take after; the important point is:
She LIGHTER!

And her nose is so fine...
Sometimes I think she is almost as pretty as ME!

And light!
I mean she, oh she sooo light and pretty.

Her nose sooo sweet too.. ..with a cute little turn up.
Not a darkie's nose at all eh?
What do you all think?

But that Marie she a nice mix if I do say so myself.
I sooo proud of how she turned out and all"

<u>DIRECTION</u>

Moira dances around as if she is the happiest woman in the world in
her anticipation.
Preening herself.

<u>MUMMY/MOIRA</u> continues:

"Any how's I'm getting rid, so I can concentrate on what's important.
And what's important is Me and Marie!
And our future...
She will get a nice English husband for true.
And Melanie can stay here where she belongs on the Island
Talking the Lingo 'till her and her precious Gran's hearts are content
eh?
She good at doing domestic stuff ...and all kinds of tings like that..

What is it the English say?
Horses for courses!

And she sure is just that ....
A good workhorse for sure. "

<u>DIRECTION</u>
Moira shakes her head in a puzzled manner.

<u>MUMMY /MOIRA</u> continues..

"Yeah... You all like animals too
All about vegetables and fruit... and then the animal ting and all..."

<u>DIRECTION</u>

Moira / Mummy stops twirling around.
She stands dead still; and becomes quietly serious.

"Trouble is that Michael seem fond of her.
TOO fond if you ask me. He want her over fuh true.

And he have these silly notions about her education and all that sort of
ting like that.

I mean she might not be pretty and all.
But!
She still a girl!
She don't need no educating...not as she set to marry some half Island
boy or some such thing.

Her Grand will set her up with some boy or other..
Someone just right for the likes of her
She'll be happy enough eh?

That Melanie, She always been a pain to me..
Right from the birth..
Oh what a birthing that was I could tell you"

DIRECTION

Moira Stops herself.. abruptly! As if she is remembering who she is
talking to.

DIALOGUE (Continues in an almost conspiratorial fashion)

"Of course being a lady I don't go into details.. of such personal things
like that..
I'll just say the pain started from the word go and to this day she ain't
letting up on me!
The very fact I was pregnant with her was bad enough.

And Men!
They always wanting a boy..
She a girl you know!
The man confused or what?

I mean what a waste and all, when she should be learning about babies and the like.

And she will have to get married if only for appearances sake.
I mean the shame of having an unmarried daughter!

And no man want a clever clogs for a wife you know!

That Melanie too uppity already without that sort of thing added on.

And that Michael's ideas making her worse.. it will be hard enough to get rid as it is!"

DIRECTION

Moira Twirls around to face Melanie.
Moira is now suddenly transformed into a happy doting Mother.

Moira walks back and sits back in her armchair.
Now back in REAL TIME

DIALOGUE

MOIRA /MUMMY (Moira's voice softens and calms down.)

"Now come on Melanie there's a good girl..
We have to get these things packed up before Daddy comes back.
We don't have much time left, and I have to get your things ready to take over to Grandma's place too!

We going in the morning...

Isn't it wonderful?
You happy and I'm happy
Which will mean Daddy happy too!

Isn't that what he is always saying?
That if we happy he happy eh?"

DIRECTION

Melanie's face reflects her acceptance, and even a wry smile appears on her face...

MELANIE

"Don't worry Mummy, everything will be ready on time, and we will ALL be happy from now on. Now, I just know it.

You and Marie can enjoy all your fanciness together.

I will look after Grandma, and you know what?
She will take care of me too"

DIRECTION

MELANIE TO THE AUDIENCE/ SUSPENSION

" And... Do You all know what?

She wins, I'm tired and it's all I can do to save me...

Maybe when she is older Marie will be able to see sense.

As Grandma says.. things will be as they will be Mel
So that's us for now"

DIRECTION
Back in REAL TIME

Mother and Daughter continue to pack, and Melanie instinctively reaches across to a side table in order to put on the radio.

Music comes on and she starts to hum to the radio.
Melanie sings/ hums a little of __Wake up To The Radio__ >

Moira/ Mummy glares at Melanie, sensing Melanie's happiness at being parted from her Mother.

The two realise their animosity is for keeps... and how in their own way(s) they are looking forward to their separate new beginnings.

MUMMY/MOIRA

"Turn that noise off!"

DIRECTION

Melanie turns off the radio.
Moira leans over as she has many times before to deliver Melanie another hard slap.
Melanie hardly reacts at all.

MOIRA / MUMMY

" There's another little something to remember me by!

You forgetting yourself Melanie!
You not with that Grandma yet"

MELANIE

" Don't worry Mummy..
You have already given me plenty to remember you by!"

DIRECTION

Melanie continues packing silently. She holds back the tears.
At this point DADDY/ Michael appears, carrying a folder...happy and excited. This Man seems oblivious to the dynamics of his family...
He seems happy and elated.

DIALOGUE

DADDY/ MICHAEL

"Aye!
So, how's my little harem getting on?

Look! I have all the papers we need, and they have even fixed us up with an apartment until we can find a house of our own ...

So we can all go together now.. There's no need for Mel to stay behind, there will be plenty of room for us all straight away"

DIRECTION

A turgid look from Moira/ Mummy in his direction stops him in full throttle!

DIALOGUE

MICHAEL / DADDY

"I mean Melanie, there's no need for Melanie to stay, we can book a flight for her too now.

There will be room for us all...heh Mel...anie!
What do you think to that?"

MELANIE

"I don't know Daddy, I'm ok with staying, what with Grandma, and Missy needing me, and I would so miss Cherie...so I don't really know..

Mummy says it's best for me to stay here..
What with London being so fancy and all...
And that it's my duty to stay here and be with Grandma, and I agree with Mummy about that bit.
Maybe about all of it."

DIRECTION

Melanie and Moira are joining forces in an unholy alliance, for their own different motives:

DIALOGUE

MUMMY/ MOIRA (Quickly interrupting)

"Now shush up child, your Daddy doing that thing again..
He has always been too soft with you...

Daddy you know full well Grandma soo fond of this child, it would be too much for her to be parted from us all, all at once you know dat is so.

Maybe it's best we do leave her here for a good while ...Kinder.

'Till such a time as we all get properly settled, just like we said."

DIRECTION

Daddy looks crestfallen and looking across to Melanie he shakes his head, his hands fall to his side and the papers fall to the floor...

DIALOGUE

MUMMY/MOIRA

"Melanie now see what you done, pick up Daddy's' papers."

DIRECTIONS

Melanie scrambles across the floor picking up Michael's papers.
She now stands up and hands them back to him.

She places her arm upon his.
They exchange looks.

MOIRA/MUMMY Continues:

"Daddy it's for the best, don't you know it will break my heart to leave her by, but I have a burden to carry, and we have to do God's will ..

And Grandma surely does need one of us here.
She soo attached to Melanie, out of all of us.
It just seems right for all round"

DADDY/ MICHAEL

"But Mummy there's plenty of family to take care of Grand ma.

We four, we should all be together now.
The girls will soon enough be off and grown from us.

110

And what about her education?
Melanie will miss out on the beginning of term and all"

MOIRA/ MUMMY

"I know Daddy I know: but that not the same..

Anyhow's you have to account for how they so close and all...
It's only for a while. We mustn't be selfish in all of this.

We will have our dear girl back just as soon as we able ...
And then she can catch up on all sorts of things like that..."

DIRECTION

Mummy begins to close some of the boxes she and Melanie have been
packing and turns again to face Melanie.
Melanie kneels back down again to continue packing, as Mel closes the
last box, she looks up at her Father.

DIALOGUE

MELANIE

"I will miss you Daddy, but Mummy is right we have to do what is
right, don't we Mummy? Especially for Grandma. "

MUMMY/ MOIRA

"Yes our daughter, we have to take care of our own,....It's our duty."

DIRECTION

Moira places one hand on Mel's shoulder: She Continues:

"I will miss you so much Melanie ..
We all will; but we have to do the right thing..
As you said, especially for dear ole Grandma "

DADDY

" Sometimes I think I will never understand any of you!"

<u>DIRECTION</u>

Daddy/ Michael is shaking his head.
He turns to leave the room, as the two women unite in their triumph
with hard looks towards one another.
When Michael has left the two women speak:

<u>MUMMY</u>

" Well Melanie that's everything wrapped up once and for all..."

<u>MELANIE</u>

"Yes, Mummy that's everything packed away, tightly until someone
opens the boxes and lets it all out again some where else."

<u>DIRECTION</u>

Moira gets up and walks across to the radio.
She re tunes it to another station.

The sounds of Big Ben's chimes come out.
A very English voice speaks from the Radio.

<u>"This is The World Service..... This is London calling......".</u>

<u>Scene Four Ends</u>

<u>SCENE FIVE Begins</u>

<u>SETTING</u>
 Grandma's homely old-fashioned kitchen in her Trinidad home.

<u>DIRECTION</u>

Opens to Grandma sitting at the table in her kitchen preparing a meal.
She has a bowl in front of her and is busily stirring something
energetically.

The table is set out in the middle of the room, with chairs around it,
with an armchair in a corner.
A Kit Kat clock is ticking away on the wall.

Grandma is content and happy now Mel and she are settled, with no
interference from the rest of the family, who are now ensconced in
London.

Melanie is out on the back porch/ gallery...she can just be seen and
heard humming, whilst sweeping up.

Grandma calls out to Melanie in a happy melodic Trinidadian voice.

<u>DIALOGUE</u>

<u>GRANDMA</u>

"Aye Mel, it makin hot fuh sure today..
Not like them over there in England eh?

They all be cold and all that..
But by now they'll all be settled well in eh Mel?
Dat Moira will be busy fuh sure, making style and all.
But we is we all right and cosied up now too eh?"

<u>DIRECTIONS</u>

Grandma stops stirring, puts down the old wooden spoon, and looks
over towards Melanie. She continues:

"It's just like them old days Mel, just like them old days...when you was teeny and all..
You always singing even in that cradle of yours' eh Mel?"

Grandma smiles to herself over the happy memories, as she continues to add to the bowl whilst stirring.

"Hah Mel you know that old film will be on that Television tonight...
I do love dem ole musicals.. and we can sing along together heh?
Yeah; Just like we always used to eh....

You done out there now?"

DIRECTION

Melanie answers by calling through to the kitchen.
Mel puts down the broom and wanders happily back <u>towards</u> the kitchen.
She is happy relaxed and at ease. Her Trini accent is to the fore.

MELANIE

"Yeah I done.

Oh Grandma, that sounds great and all, but I told Cherie I'd be going over to hers' tonight on account we have some homework and things to catch up with.."

DIRECTION

Melanie finishes up and now walks <u>into</u> the kitchen.
After speaking, Mel senses Grandma's disappointment at her words.

Mel walks over to Grandma and wraps her arms around her.

Grandma hides her momentary disappointment by shaking her head.
After all Mel is with her and that's what matters to them both.
Grandma puts on a good front, and plays down her feelings.

GRANDMA

"Oh dat's alright child, you must do your work, so you can get a good job when you go over there and all that sort of ting like that.

We can look annoder time eh"

DIRECTION

Melanie laughs and giggles still with her arms right around the frail old frame that contains the one person in the world she can always trust and love.

DIALOGUE

MELANIE

"But there again Grandma, I don't want to get too clever too quickly! Then they might want me over too soon...!

And that means we will miss watching too many movies together heh?

Time is precious Gran... isn't that what you always say?
Time and loved ones are all that really matters isn't that so Grandma?"

GRANDMA

" Now child you interfering with important work in de here and now! You getting all soppy and all that too."

DIRECTION

Grandma shakes Mel off her with a playful slap on her posteria..
She has a big grin on her old face.
Grandma goes back to stirring the contents of her bowl.

GRANDMA

"You ever heard of teaching your Grandma how to suck eggs?
I know all dat stuff fuh true...

Anyway's...
You do what you want to do, what is best for you and all.

I not telling you what to do.. it's your own business, and this, this is mine.."

Grandma shakes her wooden spoon at Melanie, and they both start to laugh again, the love and understanding between them is palpable. Mel dances about the kitchen happily, in a carefree manner. Humming nothing in particular to herself..

DIALOGUE

GRANDMA

" You dancing about again? You wear that floor out fuh sure!"

MELANIE

"Why yes of course! I'm rehearsing for tonight!
You know we always have to dance and sing when the picture on!"

GRANDMA

"I knows you always get too excited!"

MELANIE

" Well I can't think where I get that from eh Grandma?"

DIRECTION

The two laugh with one another in agreement...

GRANDMA

" Well if that's what you decided.. I not telling you different!

Your Mummy does enough telling for us all, you got to learn about growing up and making your own mistakes for your own self, and all kind of tings like that..."

MELANIE (Spoken in a comedic serious English tone)

"I couldn't agree more Grandma!

So, I declare that this is the plan.
I'll go over to Cherie's right now..
Just a bit earlier. She won't mind.
Then we can get all our work done earlier, so that I can be back for seven, at the latest.
What time does the film start? I don't want to miss a second of it! "

GRANDMA

" It tells you all in that TV paper you always buying... it over there."

DIRECTION

Grandma points to the armchair next to the stove.

GRANDMA (Continues)

"You know I not that bothered fuh true... there will be plenty more to see together yet you know."

Melanie goes across to pick up the TV Paper. She reads from the TV Magazine waving her hands about excitedly.

DIALOGUE

MELANIE

"It says here it starts at seven thirty.. so there IS plenty of time

So that's ...I mean I've decided Gran.
I shall go over to Cherie's do my work right now, and to have the chats.

Then I'll be back home in time to watch the movie with you!
So everyone will be happy eh?"

DIRECTION

Gran looks decidedly content with Mel making her decision.

DIALOGUE

<u>GRANDMA</u> (Continues)

"That's my girl.. we'll make a woman out of you yet!

But remember, your Mummy and Daddy will be telephoning tomorrow, so arrange to be in for that, otherwise there be all kind of bacchanal if you not here for dat.

That Moira sure knows how to kick up when she wants to you know. Any how you do what you do.."

<u>DIALOGUE</u>

<u>MELANIE</u> (Laughing)

" I certainly will Grandma.

Have you heard of that time management thing?
Well, that's what I'm going to follow from now on...

Not only shall I go over to Cherie's do what we have to do, and have some fun AND be back to watch the film, I will do it all again tomorrow, then be back for the call!

Maybe Cherie should come over tomorrow and we will all eat out that cook up you making too!

Your food sooo good Gran!
Heh we having roti tomorrow too or what?"

<u>DIRECTIONS</u>

Melanie picks up a spoon from the table and attempts to take some of the mixture from the bowl Grandma has been stirring.

Grandma playfully taps Melanie's hand away from the bowl

<u>GRANDMA</u>

" You stay out of that pot you hear?"

MELANIE

"So Gran you'll have to cook up a storm again tomorrow!

'Cos all of this will be gone by then eh! Don't you worry.."

DIRECTION

Grandma speaks whilst laughing and waving her spoon about..

GRANDMA

" You'll eat me out of house and home to be sure my girl!
and wear out my lino into the bargain fuh sure!

I don't know...I'll give you Time Management!

Time Management.. and all kind of fancy talk..
In my day we just used to call it getting on and dun!

Any way now, that's what I call my girl...

We'll get you all growed up for that London again, mark my words
and all,
You'll be ready with fancy talk and such.
That Mummy and Daddy won't know you when they lay eyes on you
again.."

MELANIE

" Just like last time Grandma!

I didn't really know who Mummy was when I first saw her!

Gran... This time there's no hurry is there? We is we eh?
(Said slowly and pensively)

We just fine and cosy just like you said Grandma, just like you said".

DIRECTION

With that Melanie grabs her bag from a chair.

The two share another hug and wave. And Melanie is off out of the kitchen door, running across the gallery and out across the garden. Meanwhile Grandma waves her out and looks after her.

DIALOGUE

MELANIE

"See, you before seven thirty Grandma...I promise!"

DIRECTION

Grandma begins to hum to herself...

Then:
SOMETIMES I FEEL LIKE A MOTHERLESS CHILD (Partial)

Continues and is sung From Off Stage

Scene Five Ends

SETTING the next evening:
Grandma's Comfy Old-fashioned Sitting Room.

DIRECTION

Melanie & Grandma are cosied up in the Sitting Room.

Grandma is in her favoured chair and Melanie is on the floor at her feet with her arms wrapped around Grandma's lower legs.
They have been watching the old Musical Film on the TV, and are now talking excitedly about it.

MELANIE

DIALOGUE

"I just love those old pictures Grandma, I think that one is my favourite!"

GRANDMA

"That's what you say about all of them Mel! (Laughing)
I'm glad you liked it.
See it was good to get back in time for us to see it together now wasn't it?
Tings always better when you can share them fuh true, dat what I always say anyhow"

MELANIE

"Always Grandma, it's always good, Time to free up and all.
I just love that song at the end the most.. it almost makes me cry.. just a little"

DIRECTION

Melanie gets up and begins to dance around the room.
Mel starts to hum parts of Every Day Is Like An Opera.

DIALOGUE

GRANDMA

"Mel, that's not the tune!
You usually pick up a tune fast just right and all..

But it's a lovely tune anyhow... where you get dat from eh?"

DIRECTION

Grandma gets up from her chair and together they waltz around the room... laughing gently...as Mel continues now singing a little of the words to
'Every day Is Like An Opera'.

Grandma tires, and sits back down in her chair..

DIALOGUE

GRANDMA

"Oh.. That's enough set for me!
Fuh true Mel, Where did that tune come from?

Must be some film I haven't seen?
I not heard it nowhere.
And I reckon I have seen them all one way or another."

DIRECTION

Melanie replies in a shy little voice... she speaks looking down at her feet a little.

MELANIE

"It come from inside my head Grandma,
I have lots of them whirling away inside my head "

DIRECTION

Grandma looks serious, and Melanie is wondering if she should have said about the tunes in her head. Mel is looking somewhat pensive: What will Grandma think?

DIALOGUE

GRANDMA

"Come here my child.."

DIRECTION

Grandma holds out her arms . Mel kneels back down.
Gran takes Mel's face into her hands and looks into her eyes lovingly (Showing the stark contrast to how Moira has held Mel's face in her hands)

DIALOGUE

GRANDMA

"But darling Mel that's wonderful!
That's the most wonderful gift anyone might have!

My own little Hollywood star...
Sing it to me again. I want to hear all of it fuh true".

MELANIE (Sighing, then speaking in a relieved but happy tone)

"Well I'm not too sure all the words are ready yet Grandma, but I can try"

DIRECTION

At that precise moment their time together is broken, for now and for good. The telephone rings, and the two jump a little apart as if they know the news that is coming.

Grandma gets up from her chair and walks across the room.

Meanwhile Mel is now up again and is dancing slowly to the music in her head humming softly.
Grandma lifts the receiver.
Gran talks a little louder than normal into the mouthpiece...

DIALOGUE

GRANDMA

"Hello"
(Slight Pause)

"Ah hello Moira, Yes she well, Yes She here, do you want to speak to... No? .. ah ah.....
(LONG PAUSE whilst **Moira** at the other end speaks...)

"Yes, I'll tell her. Moira. You sure?"
(Another long pause.)

"Yes I will, yes. She'll be ready and all"

DIRECTION

Grandma sighs. Mel meanwhile has slowed down her dancing and humming to almost slow motion. Mel stops as if in mid flow.

MELANIE   (In a strained voice, knowing but hoping it is not what she is fearing it is)

" Grand ma what is it?"

GRANDMA

" I think you know Darlin' I think you knows what it is..

You going home, You going back home.....
To your Mummy and your Daddy."

DIRECTION

The two stand alone across from one another. Grandma with the receiver still clasped in her hand. Mel herself is in mid slow dance.

124

Everything is slowed down as if in a dream, as when time stands still. This moment is their last carefree moment together. Ever.

DIALOGUE

<u>MELANIE</u> (Said in an emotional panicky voice...)

"But Grandma we alright, this is my home, you are my home Grandma...I don't want to go back."

DIRECTION

The two slowly merge into one as if in a dance. The music plays in the background as they slowly hold onto one another to the music.

<u>'EVERY DAY IS LIKE AN OPERA '</u>

(3/4 excerpt this time. Lush strings but quietly)

to an increasingly darkened stage.

<u>Scene Six Ends</u>

<u>SCENE SEVEN Begins</u>

<u>SETTING Plush Sitting Room in London. The James' Family Home.</u>
<u>A few weeks later:</u>

<u>DIRECTION</u>

A new Sitting Room in London.
Moira / Mummy is sitting in a comfy chair reading a Magazine,.

Melanie is walking towards the telephone by the window.
She puts her hand on the receiver, as if she is about to make a call.

Moira looks up with a cross look on her face. Melanie stops at once,
saying:

<u>DIALOGUE</u>

<u>MELANIE</u>

"Mummy , Daddy said I could..."

<u>DIRECTION</u>

Melanie does not get the chance to finish her sentence.
Moira gets up from her chair and flies across the room.

Moira pulls the receiver forcibly away from Melanie.
The receiver hits Melanie in her face, by accident or design.. It is hard
to tell.

<u>MUMMY/MOIRA</u>

<u>DIALOGUE</u>

" That's it now, you get off that 'phone, your Daddy isn't made of
money you know...I said stop!"

<u>DIRECTION</u>

Melanie is holding her face. Moira slams the telephone back firmly in
its place. Moira calms down a little; sensing she may have gone too
far.

126

MOIRA/MUMMY

" See that's what happens when you don't do as you are told straight away making me vexed and all!

(Moira walks back to her chair with a sullen face.
Moira picks up her magazine.
She sits back in her original position.)

MOIRA/MUMMY continues:

"Just go back, go back to your chores..
And stop mithering me"

MELANIE

" But Mummy I never had chance to say goodbye properly to Cherie,
and I do so miss her and I do so need to talk with Grandma..

Just for a little while.. just to hear her voice
Her voice always soothes me so.... Please say yes...
Daddy really said did say I could.. Fuh true.."

DIRECTION

Mummy/Moira glares angrily at Mel.

MELANIE

" I'm sorry, Mummy,
Sometimes I just forget. It just slips out..

But it is true, Daddy said I could.. And I just need..."

MOIRA / MUMMY (Interrupts acidly: Speaking in a shrill voice)

" Need! Need!
We all need something Melanie..
But that doesn't mean we get it.

Now you look here, I've just about had enough of this moaning.
You had best ways get used to things as they are.

127

You got a younger Sister to worry over and watch out for, so you can forget about Cherie and all.

Anyhow's you won't be seeing her again, so get used to the facts.

You here now and <u>this</u> is your home...

This is your life now, and we all have to get used to being here..
It's hard for me too you know....

Having to find things to occupy you and all.. until you married off and such..
You never think of what I having to put up with do you?
You is such a selfish girl!

I am sure I don't know where you get it from!!
You never did learn The Lords' Way
Did you?

No matter how often I drag you to Church and all kinds of things like that..
My, the time and the effort I have put into your upbringing.
Not to mention the expense!"

DIRECTION

There is now a hiatus in the tirade...
Moira looks pensive...she becomes very quiet...fussing and shifting about in her chair opening and closing up her magazine.
Then she sits silently, peering ahead in thought.

MOIRA/MUMMY

"Any ways I have something to tell you...

I've been meaning to for a while..
But we all been so busy what with one ting and annoder
The house and all kind of ting like that "

DIRECTION

Again there is a thoughtful pause..

128

Melanie now sits on the chair which is next to the 'phone.
Mel feels expectant, waiting for something, she knows not what, but
feels it won't be good news.

<u>MOIRA/MUMMY</u> Continues:

"There'll be no more Grandma being soft with you ever again.
Neither will there be such talking to Grandma...

So you had better know...
Know now I suppose.
She dead now, and that's that."

<u>DIRECTION</u>

Melanie looks stunned. She is silent.
Then appears as if she is going to cry.

<u>MOIRA</u> senses this, so in order to avoid explanations she quickly
continues:

"I tell you that's not going to happen any more.
So get used to the facts Melanie.
She dead and all. She gone.

Gone from you and everything else on dis earth now.
So you better get used to that reality too and all.

There'll be no more interfering from Grandma anymore now nor ever
more.
Now you <u>is</u> my child fuh true, alone.
With no interfering..
No more running to Grandma for sympathy and all kinds of things
like that.

Just remember I can do what I want with you anytime I WANT.
For sure...

Now you go and kneel down and think on what I told you.
Go on! Across there   (Said pointing to a corner of the room)
And let me be in peace.
Go on do as you are told."

129

DIRECTIONS

Moira points again impatiently to a far corner of the room...
Melanie stands up rigidly in shock, tears run silently down her face.

Melanie eventually walks across to where Moira has pointed.
Melanie kneels down.

Melanie can be seen sideways on by the audience.
In between sobs Melanie gains the courage to ask some questions:

MELANIE

" Why didn't you tell me Mummy? Why?

When Mummy? when?
And how come?
Grandma was fine when I left...
She was just fine.."

DIALOGUE

MUMMY / MOIRA

"You stupid girl

What you are you talking about ?
I just did.
I told you now, so don't start up again.

There ain't nothing can be done about it.

She gone and that's that.
That's what happens when you ole..
One minute you here the next you gone...

There's no need for any fuss and all kinds of thing like that..
She just gone to meet her Maker... that's all..."

DIRECTION

There is a deathly silence between the women.

Moira can see she might have gone too far again.
In some panic her anger increases, making things worse.

DIALOGUE

" Now don't you dare go bothering your Daddy with all of this..
You hear now!

Nor Marie nor anybody else come to that.

We don't need any more expense right now, you know..

The rest of the family over there can take care of all of that...
We tell Daddy soon enough when everything is done with.
Anyhow she not his Mother..

He'll be told when he need to know."

MELANIE

" Mummy maybe if I stayed a while longer Grandma would have been
alright...
Like you said it was my duty to stay and look after her.
Then _you_ brought me here!"

MOIRA/MUMMY (Said with an ironic laugh)

" Huh! What difference could you have made! You stupidee.
And don't you go kidding yourself Melanie!
It was Daddy who brought you here not me..

What are you thinking about?

If it had been up to me you would have stayed there forever with your
ole precious Grandma!
I'm telling you now!"

DIRECTION

Moira gets up from her chair again and aims her hand at the back of
Melanie's head..

MOIRA/MUMMY

"No one is interested in you now Melanie.. NO – ONE!
(Moira turns away from Melanie…)

You know Melanie you is so ugly right now that meh can't bear to be
in the same room as you when you are like this and all.

If you so worried about this and all..
Just stay still and pray for your precious Grandma's soul.

I can tell you she will need your prayers and all, if she going to get
any chance to be getting into Heaven!
She never in Church or nothing that woman..
Why I had to practically train myself in the way of The Lord!

What kind of Mother was that to me? Eh
I ask you..
I was let down badly eh?

And you, you so lucky.. And never once have I been thanked for all
my efforts .. Never once!

So Pray, Pray hard Melanie!
For both your souls eh!

I'll know if you move, and God will know too, so you stay there 'till I
come and get you.. you stay there fast!

I need some peace from all of this mess up
I'm going to my bedroom…

And you!
You stay away from that telephone you hear me!
Anyhow you soon won't have any one to call at all..

Cherie will soon tire of you,
She probably got better friends than you already eh?
And her parents, they will tire of those stamp and telephone bills and
all kinds of things like that"

DIRECTION

132

Moira / Mummy flounces out of the room leaving the door open.

There is a prolonged **SILENCE** whilst Melanie continues to kneel half-facing the wall.
Melanie is now trembling and sobbing whilst remembering her Grandma.

Then Melanie stands up and walks centre stage to defiantly sing the **FULL** version of

'SOMETIMES I FEEL LIKE A MOTHERLESS CHILD'

DIRECTION

Mid way **GRANDMA** appears at the doorway which Moira left by.

Grandma has her arms stretched out to Melanie like she used to.

Grandma is silently mouthing to Mel.. But she cannot be heard, whilst Mel is singing.
Eventually Melanie begins to sense Grandma's presence.

When the song is finished Melanie calls out, and peers towards the doorway.

Now Mel feels and thinks she can see Grandma.
Melanie is sobbing intermittently.

DIALOGUE

MELANIE

"Gran.
Grandma is that you?
Gran are you there?

Your Jumbie Grandma?
Are you with me?

I never got to say goodbye!"

133

Mel is now ready and able to see **Grandma's Spirit**:

GRANDMA (**Grandma's Spirit/ Jumbie** can now be heard)

" Don't cry child..

We don't ever need to say goodbye you know

I will always watch over you..
I will always hear you singing out to me

I just a bit farther away now that's all..

Just a bit further away

I will always love you Mel always…..Fuh true

You not alone
You never alone now Mel
Heh girl we don't need that telephone now..

We connected forever Mel
Forever. All you have to do is tune in Mel.

Just tune in"

DIRECTION

Grandma is now fading until she can no longer be seen.
She is gone.

Melanie walks across the room in order to kneel back down in the same
corner turning her face to the wall.
Melanie sobs quietly with her head down into her chest.

Then:

BLACK SILENT STAGE

Scene Seven Ends

<u>SCENE EIGHT Begins</u>

<u>SETTING. London Schoolyard.</u>

<u>DIRECTION</u>

Opens in a schoolyard.
There are lots of Teenage and younger Girls milling around.
A little crowd has grown around Marie and Melanie.

Melanie is sitting on the bench with her younger sister Marie who is
crying. Mel has her arms around her and is looking up at the melee
surrounding them.

Melanie has been sent to collect Marie from school.
Mel stands up and begins to push a few girls away from the bench and
from her Sister.

<u>DIALOGUE</u>

<u>MELANIE</u>

"Just leave her alone..
Marie's not used to some things around here that's all."

<u>FIRST TEENAGE GIRL (CARRIE)</u>

"So what's it to you then?
You not from this school, as a matter of fact you not from 'round here
at all...
You looks like you some kind of Nurse or other...
What is it? she got her Nursey here to look after her or what? "
(Said teasingly)

<u>MELANIE</u>

" I tell you what it's to do with me ... I'm her Sister!
And I <u>am</u> from 'round here, I was born just down the road, if you want
to know!
And I am here to take care of my Sister....So there.

And what's more I'm no Nanny nor Nurse.... Neither."

135

The Teenage girl (<u>Carrie</u>) takes a step back as the crowd begins to grow..
Carrie seems less sure of her ground now she has been challenged, and she begins to back-track her stance a little.

<u>TEENAGE GIRL (CARRIE)</u>

"Any ways' I bet your Mum's a Nurse, and you will be in the future...
that's what you lot do...
Take care of other people's kids and all that sort of stuff"

MELANIE

DIALOGUE

"What are you on about?
Who is you lot? You look like 'you lot' yourself eh?

And what's all this about Nurses?
Nurses: what's wrong with being a Nurse anyhow?"

First TEENAGE GIRL (CARRIE)

"You lot...is...you all cleaners and stuff like that innit?
All you Jamaicans, they all Nurses or some such thing...

We aspire to greater things 'round here you know...
Don't we Betsy?"

DIRECTIONS

At this Carrie turns to the crowd looking for support...

A few of them start to giggle, but one or two look uneasy, until another girl pipes up>>>

DIALOGUE

SECOND TEENAGE GIRL (BETSY)

" Ease up Carrie, what you on earth you on about anyhow?
You Dad Jamaican himself innit?
So what does that make you? You ijit!

Any how......Some of us have Mums who are Nurses,
Like me for instance!

You want to make something of it? eh?
And like she says there's nothing wrong with that...

Leave her alone she's only looking out for her little kid Sister...
Leave her be"

THIRD TEENAGE GIRL (JOANIE)

" Yeah Carrie leave her be, she only doing what a lot of us 'round here
have to do; taking care of the little ones, we all got Mum's who have to
work and stuff..."

DIRECTIONS

At this point Marie gets a little braver and decides to join in as she
feels the tide has turned to her and Melanie's favour.

Everyone now seems to be talking at once, when a voice penetrates the
din. Marie gets up to shout out over the general melee!

DIALOGUE

MARIE

" What you all talking about? I'm NOT little...
Am I Mel?"

DIRECTIONS

At this point everyone stops talking..
There is a Silence..
Everyone stares at Marie and then laughter breaks out.

The new friendships In London are about to begin.

MELANIE

" No Marie, you're not little at all.. in fact you beginning to be quite grown up…"

DIRECTIONS

Mel gives Marie a small hug, which Marie shuns and accepts simultaneously (not wanting to appear too reliant on her big sister in front of the others).

The girls recover from their laughter and begin to talk a while. Joanie is the first to start asking Melanie questions as the two sit back on the bench.

Meanwhile Marie wanders off to the side with some of the younger girls, who have pulled her over to them.
They are heard gently laughing as they share hair fancies…

Betsy then joins up with Mel and Joanie on the bench.

DIALOGUE

JOANIE (Said to Melanie)

" Sorry about all that Carrie can be a bit stupid some times…"

DIRECTION

CARRIE is feeling a bit put - out now. She is lingering over by the wall behind the bench…with a few older girl stalwarts of hers.

Carrie and these girls continue to stand about occasionally pushing one another when making a point.

DIALOGUE

CARRIE

" I heard that…!

I'm not stupid … I know what's what.

My Mum says it always pays to know who you are dealing with.
To protect yourself from newcomers and such, until you know what
they about "

JOANIE (Ignoring Carrie)

"As it happens my Mum, she come over from Jamaica, least I think she
did.. I dunno..
Maybe she born here not there.. or she came over when she little...well
whatever.. Truth is I can't remember what the oldies told me!
Look ... the fact is we nearly all have parents or Grans' that come over
from some place else...

One way or another ..
So what of it eh?

Ain't that right Betsy?"

DIRECTION (Joanie then turns her attention back again to Melanie.)

JOANIE (Continues)

"Anyhow Betsy here easy! She got the complete set!

The rest of us, we a mixed bag.. But we all of us born here too!
Just like you say you was! Well mostly...

Anyhow; what's your name then?
And where are you really from?
It's just ...

We not seen you 'round here before
I mean if you not..

Aren't you a Jamaican?"

DIRECTIONS

This is the question Melanie is to face for the rest of her life.
At this point she realises maybe she should make a stand.

DIALOGUE

139

MELANIE

" OK. Right..   (Mel takes a big breath)

I'm called Mel...
Short for Melanie, but only my Mum calls me that! Which I hate!

And over there that's my Sister Marie..
Which I guess you all already know..

We are both British.
In fact I'm English, I was born in LONDON
We both were.."

DIRECTIONS

The girls all go quiet. Until Carrie breaks the silence.

DIALOGUE

CARRIE

" See I tell you...Joanie! We've got a right one here"

MELANIE

" Look it's simple...for example..
Carrie where did you say your parents from?"

CARRIE

" Well that's easy my Dad is from Jamaica ... so that makes me
Jamaican! I guess...? "

MELANIE

" And your Mum?"

CARRIE

"She's a Londoner from Canning Town innit!
Me! I'm a Londoner through and through!"

BETSY (To Carrie)

"Any how's you born here Carrie so dat makes you British!
Don't it Mel?"

JOANIE

" Well my folks were born here, So I KNOW what I am... 'Cos My
Dad's white and all..

Even though my Gran from Jamaica..

But my Mum can't remember Jamaica too well as she say she only
visited, and she always lived in Notting Hill innit.

Though as I said.. Maybe she born ...Oh I don't know really!

 What do say to that Mel?"

DIRECTIONS

The girls all look to Mel....As if: Well, she started all of this..

Then Carrie pipes up..
Still maybe looking to usurp Mel a little from her dominating the
conversation.

DIALOGUE

CARRIE

" Yes all knowing one..
 What do you say about all of this...
You who aren't a Jamaican...

I mean Betsy here she all Black
Her parents from Jamaica for true

141

So she must be Jamaican innit?"

DIRECTIONS

Mel considers for a moment sensing her position and budding
friendships could be in jeopardy..
She decides to take the reins and to sort this out once and for all.
Mel begins to talk again; tentatively...

DIALOGUE

MELANIE

"I think...   (Pause)   I think...."

CARRIE (Walking over to be even closer to the three girls on the bench)

" Yeah we get that! ....
You think.
We all think; but what do you think Miss Philosopher?

I don't think you know what you think other than you aren't a Jam... "

BETSY

" Carrie don't start that up again!.
 Mel here, she's just gathering her thoughts...
Ain't you Mel?

Anyhow I born here too.
Don't know anywhere else me..
I've not even been out of London ever...
So this is my patch for sure!

Though I could have, if I'd gone on that School trip...

My Mum said my Dad would come up with the readies..
But he never did.."

DIRECTIONS

Betsy's voice trails off...

Mel looks fondly on to Betsy and puts her arm around her.

MELANIE

" Thanks Betsy, I just think"...

CARRIE

" Oh No. Not again! .
If you ask me....She doesn't know what she thinks..

She's the one who is stupid not me!
I'm not wasting any more of my time on this rubbish stuff "

DIRECTIONS

Carrie is sensing victory and begins to walk away, chunnering to
herself, strutting a little...
Maybe she is sensing some sort of triumph.

Melanie gets up from the bench to chase a little after Carrie,
Leaving Joanie and Betsy sitting.

MELANIE

DIALOGUE

" No wait Carrie don't be like that.
I do know what I think..
Look.
Since I got back to London all sorts of things have happened to me.
All sorts of people have looked at me like they know who I am, what I
am.
Sometimes like I don't belong! Like I shouldn't be here..

But now I have no place else to be!
Even all of you judged me to be who and what I'm not.

All I am saying is I am Me.
Mel.
And you all are you, no matter who your parents are, or where THEY
may or may not have been from once.

I just know I am here, and this is where I was born and where I belong, and where I am now.

And more importantly where I'm going to stay..
Where I have the right to be, and maybe it's already getting to be all I know now..

I don't know...
And so. Well maybe that's who you all are too?"

DIRECTIONS

The three girls look puzzled and start to shuffle about looking at their feet feeling a bit embarrassed... not knowing why?

MELANIE continues >

"What I am saying is we aren't going back any where's and this is where we are, and partly who we are going to be.

So. We are British aren't we?
Or maybe English?

Well, we're definitely Londoners!"
(Said whilst looking towards Betsy)

DIRECTIONS

The extended group continue to look puzzled and apprehensive, but they start to gather closer around Melanie ....

DIALOGUE

CARRIE

" We don't need all of this, Me! I KNOW who I am,
I am Jamaican, and proud of it
Any ways they don't want the likes of us here.
We all of us know that, everyday, they stabbing us and stuff like dat, and covering it all up too!"

BETSY

"You need to make your mind up what you are girl!
You were a Londoner a minute ago innit?

You proper Jamaican now eh?"

MELANIE

" Carrie Look I know it's difficult...
It's the same for all of us

I'm not saying you not Jamaican..
Like I'm not saying I'm not Trinidadian

I'm not saying you shouldn't be proud of it, being Jamaican!
BUT what I am saying is this is your home too.. our home too!

So what does it matter what 'they' want..

This is our London just as much as "theirs"
Things have changed you know!

And maybe we have to change along with things too eh?
We new people, we not our parents
Thank God! I got meh own DNA innit! (Copying the local speech)

And Me!
Well I'm proud of and love where my parents come from too..

But ME I'm here.
I'm here in the now. Not in the past where I might have once been.

I here in Britain...

Look I've written a song.
It helps me sometimes to make sense of it all.
We could sing it now if you'd like....

It's funny.
I mean loads of white people think if you Black you IS Jamaican.
Like there are no other possibilities.

145

I mean why, even you lot…"

CARRIE (Relenting a little)

" Well I suppose you got a point…
Anyhow, you don't look good enough to be a Jamaican,

Come to think of it, I don't know why anyone would ever think you
are!"

DIRECTION

There is some muted slightly embarrassed laughter, and a looking
down at and shuffling of feet.

The ice has finally been broken. The girls look sheepish and begin to
push one another around gently in fun.

CARRIE

"Anyhow I bet the song is rubbish!"

MELANIE

" Rubbish! How dare you! (Laughing)

It's brilliant..
Come on I'll teach you.. All of you.

Get up. Let's celebrate our DNA! (Said whilst pulling Betsy & Joanie up
from the bench)

And then we can dance to it too! I love to dance. Don't you all?"

DIRECTION

The younger girls now start to turn around to take notice.
They form an outer circle looking on.

BETSY

"Come on then let's practice.. You never know we could end up on TV!"

JOANIE

"Yeah. Let's give it a go... It'll be a laugh!"

DIRECTIONS

The groups of girls start to laugh nervously.
MELANIE begins to teach them the song. The older girls start to join in, then quickly build up and get into the song (and dance)

'BUT AREN'T YOU A JAMAICAN?' (FULL Vocal Version)

They all stand in a line...

MELANIE starts to sing, the girls do the chorus and 'answer back' sections.

Eventually the younger group all join in too; including the smallest ones.

SET DANCE ROUTINE

The scene ends with the most of the two groups hugging together, with laughter and happiness.

SCENE Eight Ends

<u>SCENE NINE Begins</u>

<u>SETTING JAMES' FAMILY HOME, SITTING ROOM LONDON.</u>

<u>DIRECTION / SET</u>

The scene opens back in the James' London home in their sitting room.

MELANIE is in her night gown sitting watching whilst Mummy (MOIRA) and Daddy (MICHAEL) are busy attending to the last minute touches to the groaning drinks and buffet table set up in a corner of the room. There is much fussing about. Mainly from Moira.

The table is filled with Trinidadian Foods;
Such as Corn Pie, Chicken Pelau, Roti, Dahl and Plantain.

A fruit punch is in the middle of the table, as Pride of place; together with coconut water, carrot juice, mauby, soursop or sorrel as alternative drinks to the sides.

Moira and Michael are both dressed to 'impress'

To the other side of the room there is a sideboard housing a c.d. player... together with speakers, assorted CD's and a few old cassette tapes.

<u>DIALOGUE</u>

<u>MUMMY / MOIRA</u>

" It is a fine spread even if I do say so myself...
And that fruit punch is just right for all ages...creates the right impression as they say.
Very proper, very proper indeed eh Michael?"

<u>DIRECTION</u>

Michael doesn't answer other than give Moira a quizzical pained stare. Moira is surveying the scene in a very smug and self-satisfied manner. Mummy/ Moira is now making it plain that Melanie should be making herself scarce.

<u>MUMMY/MOIRA</u>

"We all done here now Melanie.
There's nothing left here for you to do.
There'll be plenty you can help with in the morning..
I know how you like to help out, doesn't she Daddy?

That her forte isn't that what they say?
Isn't it?
She very domesticated.

Don't you think so Daddy?"
She not as good as you think she is at school chores you know.."

MELANIE

"Mummy, no - one calls school work chores!"

MOIRA/ MUMMY

"It's no matter what they're called..
You not that good in school is all I saying Melanie..
I tink yuh best at recess fuh sure eh?"

DIRECTION

Moira chuckles a little at her own 'joke'

"Any ways, So.
You will need to be good at chores in the house
For your future.. and all "

MICHAEL / DADDY

"Dat not true Mummy... she better than most in school....Ease up yuh
mout some...You do so harp on like dat, and it ain't true yuh know!
I wish you not so keen to put her down all the time there Mummy yuh
know!

But for true Mel.. anie, she kind too an always keen to help anyone
out, Yes, She got a kind heart.. just like her Gran...

But she got a good head on her shoulders too yuh know.

149

As I say; she just like her ole Grandma in many respects.
Ah deh always had some rale good rapport those two eh Moira?"

DIRECTION

Michael shakes his head sadly..
He and Melanie exchange sad looks..

DIALOGUE

MOIRA/ MUMMY (Is feeling she needs to change the subject back to the imminent party. Moira begins to speak again in a conciliatory manner)

" Come.. Come now Daddy..
 I don't mean nuttin you know dat and such eh?

And ...We don't want to talk of such things now....do we?
Nor of sad things now do we?

Not when we all looking forward so to such a nice time and all.
Party and such.

So Melanie dear you had better make yourself scarce now, before anyone arrives.

And mind you keep an eye on your sister now, as I've told you to.

And call in on her now and then, just to check she is all right.

Come on now hurry up..
I said you best get yourself out of the way now...

I don't want you being seen in your night -dress and all".

MELANIE

" Well it's you who made me put this on, like I'm a child, sending me to bed at this time..

I could stay and help..
Help out with the drinks and play the music maybe, "

MUMMY / MOIRA

"Hush up now... And get along,

I told you already, you _can_ help but in the morning, clearing up.
There will be plenty for you to do then and all"

DADDY /MICHAEL

" She got a point you know Mummy, she could hang around a bit at
the beginning and meet folk, maybe help out a little..."

MUMMY / MOIRA (Turning nasty for a second speaking sharply,
then relenting)

" And who gonna look after the little one?

(Now with a softened voice/ changing tack once again)

Daddy dear understand eh?

I can't be the perfect hostess like in the magazines _and_ tend to Marie in
the night and all that sort of thing like that...

What if she wakes up with a bad dream? or some such thing?

No Daddy, it's Melanie's duty to take care of her Sister just like I did
when I her age...

Anyhow; what would _she_ say to such folk?
She would just embarrass herself and you..
She know nuttin to talk about yet with such folk!

And even if she did
You know sometimes she talks Lingo... a real Trini English mash up
that no-one can understand!"

DIRECTION

DADDY/ MICHAEL looks down as Melanie walks to the doorway, he
continues to protest a little half heartedly..

DADDY/MICHAEL

" Marie not a baby yuh know, who needs taken care of in the night nowadays!

And Melanie.. She's a good girl Moira.
She wouldn't embarrass no one.

A little bit of dancing... (Michael dances around as a little demonstration) Is a good thing for a young lady to do... yuh know.. In preparation for when she older..

Maybe it wouldn't hurt if she put on a pretty dress just for a short while and joined in a little... just for an hour or so...she very good at working that CD player an all..."

MUMMY/MOIRA

" I dare say she is, that's because she had too much practice at it !...

You shouldn't encourage her so...
I'll have to see that stops.. too much time wasted listening to music...she takes after you... encouraging her with all that sort of thing like that and all...

Melanie has to get used to doing chores, cooking and such... not that kind of thing! That be of no use to her in de future yuh know!

There'll be some young man can do that tonight...she got to know her place and all".

MICHAEL / DADDY

(Michael has been dancing around light heartedly all this time whilst Moira was speaking.
He now stops literally in his tracks. His mood and voice darkens:
He now speaks angrily:)

" And exactly what place is that Moira?
She not a servant you know...

She is my daughter is she not?"

152

DIRECTION

PAUSE.

THEN **MOIRA** speaks to the audience (Said in her best Queen's English accent: Whilst slipping in and out of Trini.)

MOIRA / MUMMY TO THE AUDIENCE / IN SUSPENSION

"Let me explain/ translate to all of you's out there who may not be Trini...Or even Jamaican for that matter!

This is what you might call a pregnant pause!
Now I shall have to nurture the status quo
With a little flattery......be boldfaced. (I good at that.)

Men sooo susceptible to a little flattery
Don't you think?

It's surprising how these immigrants pick up the language isn't it?
I'll be running the country next!

OH! What a horrifying thought!" (Said to an imaginary person as an aside, with the back of her hand to her mouth. Use extra English accent)

(Pause)

MOIRA (Continues to the audience)

"Soon you won't be able to tell the difference between us!
Apart from the obvious that is.
But we can all blend up a little and get rid of that eh?
You like that idea? Maybe so, maybe not so.
It hard to tell from your faces?"

DIRECTION Back in the Now.

MOIRA goes across to MICHAEL and puts her arm around him...in a slightly coquettish manner..

Melanie hovers by the door in case Daddy can change Moira's mind.

DIALOGUE

MOIRA / MUMMY

" Now come on Michael, don't spoil this for me, for us..
It's our big night, we in our new home with our new friends and
neighbours!

We want to make a good impression with the neighbours and our work
colleagues and all...now don't we?
These people wit influence and such yuh know.

We have to make our way in England. We in their place yuh know...
We here under sufferance... it their place fuh true.
We have to be on our best behaviour fuh sure.

And don't forget, some folk from the Church are coming along too...
We don't want any slip up's now do we?"

MICHAEL (Trying to cut in)

" But Moira, dat all nonsense...I don't need to kotow to no – one yuh
know. I as good as the next man!"

MOIRA (Ignores this and motors on without coming up for breath)

"And you know Melanie can be; well a bit odd sometimes.
You know clumsy and all that...

I am sure next time, when she's grown up a little more... a bit more
mature in her ways...Your idea will be just right.

It's just the timing
She not quite ready, That's all.
You know I want the best for her too...
Don't you?

And we do still have to think of Marie, she still a little nervy you
know, what with all the changes she has had to put up with... new
home, new school and all..

154

Anyhow, listen up, it seems we too late to change our plans now!"

DIRECTION

At this point the doorbell rings... and Michael jumps up and away from Moira's hold.

He immediately heads for the door as if programmed to respond. Looks of defeat are exchanged between Michael and Melanie.

Melanie scurries to the stairs and runs half way up before any one might see her, only just escaping from view in time.

Simultaneously, Michael opens the door and a small crowd of assorted (White & Black) folk noisily come in carrying flowers and the occasional bottle...

This influx Includes **MIRANDA** and **Three Young Men**, two of whom are white and one being mixed.
The party is set to begin.
Moira puts on her public shiny smiley face, together with her ultra perceived best English accent.
There is now a loud Melee of voices.

However in her excitement, Moira's voice rises above all others...

DIALOGUE

MOIRA / MUMMY (Said happily to all in general, together with outstretched hands. In her best English accent)

" Welcome, welcome to our lovely home come in, come in...

Soo nice to see you all...

How kind of you; thank you so much.. (Said whilst accepting some small gifts from the influx.)

How lovely"

MIRANDA (Said whilst handing Moira some flowers)

155

" Moira how lovely your home is!
I thought these might remind you of your true home!
Do you have the right vase to put them in?"

MOIRA

" So very kind of you Miranda. So thoughtful.
Please come in; help yourself to a drink."

DIRECTION

Moira smells the flowers whilst guiding Miranda over to the drinks table.
Moira instinctively hands the flowers to Michael, as one might to a servant.
Michael soon becomes over laden with various gifts from other guests, as Moira intermittently continues to off load onto him.

Michael copes as best he can by placing most things on an already over laden table..

He smiles weakly at Miranda who does not return his smile.

Whilst Miranda gazes quizzically at the proffered drinks, Moira then immediately homes in on the three young boys....

MORIA / MUMMY

" Now which one of you fine boys would like to work this CD player...?

We have a lovely selection of music, and I'm sure you will find something to your liking throughout the evening eh?

And of course, help yourselves to our spread...

We have a lovely suitable Fruit Punch as our centrepiece!
And there is sour sop and such as alternatives.
I know how you young uns love the soursop!

(Pointing to the food and drinks table, waving her hands somewhat theatrically)

Just help yourself to whatever takes your fancy boys...
Just take whatever pleases you to take!"

DIRECTION

Moira now turns her full attention back to Miranda helping her to
choose her drink. Finally Moira takes a glass and fills it with punch
for Miranda.
Miranda takes a sip, pulls a face, and they continue to chat almost
privately: whilst Michael answers the door to yet more guests arriving.

Meanwhile the three young men walk straight across to the CD player.

They immediately start to look through the music..

There is a constant melee/ hum of background chatter.

FIRST BOY (White. Whispered to other two)

DIALOGUE

"Thank God I brought some decent music...and some booze...

(He taps the side of his jacket and they all start to snigger)

Other wise we would be stuck all night on that sour sop muck... or
whatever it's called
Look at this lot.   (Said as he looks at the music, drink and food)

Some bloody Calypso shit if I'm not mistaken, Caribbean muck to eat,
and all washed down with bloody fruit juices!"
(Said as he looks across particularly to the Fruit punch)

SECOND BOY MIXED (Replies. Still whispering)

" Maybe there is some Soca? That's not too..."

(His voice fades away in the embarrassment that he even knows what
Soca is.. ..Never mind likes it)

DIRECTION

(The two other boys now stare at him in disdain.
He quickly attempts to cover up.)

"Not that I'm interested in that rubbish!

(He flushes up, and quickly changes the subject…)

Heh, I heard they've got an older daughter!
By all accounts she's a looker… for her sort anyhow…I mean.."

<u>THIRD BOY</u> (Other White Boy)

" I bet she's here somewhere… and <u>she</u> did say:

(This is said mimicking Moira's voice, keeping his voice down)

'Help yourselves to whatever takes your fancy boys'…
and I fancy…….(He laughs creepily)

I bet there's some rum in the house too…that's what they drink isn't it?
If we can find both we're well in!" (Said a bit louder.. a bit too loud?)

<u>FIRST BOY</u>

" Keep your voice down…
We don't want the old witch to hear us now do we?
Anyhow you're damn right! I hear those black girls are real goers…"

<u>THIRD BOY</u>

" Her old man would probably sell her to you for a bottle of rum…
Though it looks as if she (Pointing his head towards MOIRA)

<u>THIRD BOY</u> (Continues:)

As if she keeps him on a tight leash"
(The two white boys start to laugh.
The mixed boy looks uncomfortable.)

<u>SECOND BOY MIXED</u> (Now feeling very uncomfortable)

" Look I don't want any trouble!

And that's not a nice thing to say…
It's nasty and stupid!"

DIRECTION

The Two white boys go silent and threatening in manner.
They look at him with a very cold threatening stare.

There is a stand off for a moment.

A bit of slight, discreet amount of pushing occurs from the first white
boy to the second boy (mixed). Then the tension dissipates:

FIRST BOY

" Heh what's wrong with you.. Can't you take a joke?
You getting all sensitive or what?

We're only having fun… That's what parties are for isn't it?
Well it is where I come from!
I don't know about you!

Even parties with old codgers like this!
You got to make the most of your chances Eh?"

(Said whilst turning to the other white boy looking for support.)

THIRD BOY

" Maybe he is coming over all black or something.
You know what with being here amongst his own kind!

Have we offended your black sensitivities then eh? Have we then?"

SECOND BOY MIXED *(Delivered in a very troubled manner.*
Also, in an attempt to get back into the fold?)

" Just shut up!
I'm not bloody black…Do I look black to you? Eh? Well do I?

I Just don't want any trouble….. That's all. Just keep it down..
Now let's go and find that booze…

159

Your bottle won't last the whole night...

And I bet she's around here somewhere... (Said looking around)
Maybe she's upstairs?

Anyhow, we'll find her after we've had a few? Eh,
Then we'll have some real fun eh?"

FIRST BOY (With a smirk, and much back slapping of Mixed Boy)

" Now that's more like it.
That's our boy...
You had me worried for a while..
I thought you were going over to the dark side or something!
Yeah, we'll have a good nosy 'round later when we've had a few..
This lot won't miss us. "

DIRECTION

They all begin to laugh quite loudly.
They put arms around one another in an exaggerated manner.
Aping a comradely fashion.

ALL THREE BOYS

"Come on. Let's show this lot how to party"

The three boys walk across to the drinks table to pour out a tiny bit of
fruit juice, whilst **The First Boy** surreptitiously adds some liquor from
his jacket pocket into their drinks.

DIRECTION

MOIRA

Still in her happy mode, and still with Miranda, Moira turns her head
as she hears the boys laughing. Moira is of course oblivious to the
snarky comments.

DIALOGUE. MOIRA

" It sounds as if the party doing well already Miranda eh?

The boys seem happy enough!
Come, let me introduce you to my Husband properly"

DIRECTION

Moira guides Miranda over towards Michael. Moira places her hand on the arm of her Premium Prized guest, like she has a prize she doesn't want to let go of. Moira is beaming with pride (about the coup that is Miranda!)
Miranda doesn't look too pleased with neither the personal contact, nor the suggestion.

MOIRA

"Michael dear, do let me introduce to you my dear colleague Miranda...
Remember her?
You have often heard me talk so well of her?
How she has made me feel so welcomed at work and such...
I feel as if we frens already eh? Miranda"

DIRECTION

All this is said in a proud tone and best English accent.
Together with Trini ' moments'.

MIRANDA *(Now inescapably face to face with Michael)*

DIALOGUE *(Making the best of the situation)*

" How nice to meet you..
You are as I imagined you would be.

Moira has told me so much about you..
Although I have to admit I was surprised when Moira told me your address.
I was intrigued. I just had to come! To see for myself.

I mean it is such a nice neighbourhood...
Such a lovely house too. So intriguingly tastefully done!
Though I expect it was all furnished and decorated out before you came along. Am I right? "

DIRECTION

Michael has his hand out.
Miranda ignores it, as she talks rapidly on.
As if following her train of thought, as in thinking out loud.

At this, together with the comments made:
Michael withdraws his hand.
They understand one another immediately...
Whilst Moira seems totally oblivious to the insults.

DIALOGUE

MICHAEL

" So Miranda, Just where is it you expected us to be living then?

As you know so much about me you will know me not scrunting,
Me not sweeping your road's yuh know..."

DIRECTION

Michael is deliberately taking on a Trini sound as a means of
rebellion, against Moira's 'fronting' ways.

At this point Moira is flustered and embarrassed and she hurriedly
guides Miranda away from Michael walking quickly towards the
other guests... who have lately arrived. Moira looks angrily at Michael.

Michael stands dumbfounded..
He can be heard muttering to himself...

DIALOGUE

MICHAEL / DADDY (To himself and partially to the audience)

" Bloody hell woman what's wrong wit you?
I sick of all this frontin' and such like

Can't you see nutten that is going on?
I need a rum...All this teetotal business and all

I need to take dis family in hand and no mistake...
Maybe I got it all wrong?

Moving back and all....
I only wanting to do what's best for us all..
And maybe what I have done is what's all wrong"

DIRECTION

Michael stands alone shaking his head sadly.

Meanwhile Moira is fronting and beaming. She wafts over to the 'boys' urging them to find some music to play ...

At this point Michael leaves the room.. Still muttering under his breath.
Moira enthusiastically suggests some soft pan music to the boys.

DIALOGUE

MOIRA

" Now you boy's I hear you laughing and all, having a good time eh?
Maybe we should play some Pan to keep your spirits up high eh?
There's nothing like it you know for such spirits.
Yes we famous for it.

You know the famous steel pan?
It was invented in Trinidad yuh know."

(Moira is forgetting herself for a moment.)
Maybe it is the anticipation of the music.
Her Trinidadian accent seeps back to the fore.)

DIRECTION

Moira finds and puts on her favoured Pan c.d. to the dismay of her guests who mainly sport a pained expression as some **Soft Pan Music** emanates from the c.d. player.
(Use parts of **'Live Without Fear'**).

Moira begins to waft around gently yet uninhibitedly for a moment to the music.

DIALOGUE

MICHAEL (Heard from off stage)

" Damn it and all to hell.
Insulted in my own home!"

MIRANDA (TO THE AUDIENCE / All else is in Suspension)

(Said to the background of Moira wafting around to the same Soft Pan Music / Parts of Live Without Fear.

" These people always revert to type you know!
Only here for a few minutes and we have to suffer something called bloody pan music.
Whatever that is..
Sounds awful to me.

What do you think?

They'll all be limbo dancing in grass skirts next..

Or is that somewhere else?

Anyhow, bloody Jamaicans...
Or whatever they are.

They're all the same
I have to say this though I was shocked to find them in a neighbourhood like this!
What were they thinking?
The poor neighbours..

There will be some for sale signs up pretty tout suite
I can tell you..(Looking around)

As I thought!
No neighbours I can see at this so-called party
It's outrageous!

But I just _HAD_ to come! I wouldn't miss this spectacle for the world!"

MOIRA

DIRECTION (Back to real time)

Moira walks across to Miranda.

DIALOGUE

MOIRA

" I am so pleased you could come tonight Miranda.
I just know we are going to be the greatest of friends!

MIRANDA

" Why Moira dear, I wouldn't miss this for the world. I can safely say
that hand on heart.

Where else would I get such entertainment?

I can't wait to tell everyone at work everything about it..
And I mean everything"

SCENE Nine Ends

DIRECTION FADE> > > > > To Pan Music
(Use Parts of 'Live Without Fear')

<u>SCENE TEN Begins</u>

<u>SETTING: MELANIE'S BEDROOM. The same night as THE Party progresses.</u>

<u>DIRECTION</u>

The stage is <u>almost</u> a black out.
It opens on to a bedroom dimly lit by a child's 'fairy' night-light, which is placed a little away from the bed.
Therefore the bed area is almost pitch black.

Someone (Melanie) is lying in the bed well covered; apparently asleep.

There is a soft tap at the door.
The door opens inwards.

Noises of laughter and clinking of glasses and the soft beat of <u>Pan</u> music (Use **Parts of 'Live Without Fear'**) playing quite muffled in the background, can just be made out.

The door closes and the sounds can no longer be heard.

The audience can just make out that a Male figure has entered the room and closed the door very quietly and carefully behind him.
He creeps across the room, almost silently, apart from a creaking floorboard.

It is impossible to make out who it is.

The audience can now just make out that
The figure has reached over to the bed. Melanie stirs a little.

The following dialogue is uttered in a whisper.

<u>DIALOGUE</u>

<u>MALE</u>

"Shush now don't be scared."

<u>(PAUSE)</u>

166

"You is missing out on all the fun being all alone up here!
What you need is a little company"

DIRECTION

The intruder eases himself quietly, even gently down onto the bed,
pushing Mel slightly to one side.

Melanie wakes up properly with a start.
Melanie raises her head a little from her sleeping position.

MELANIE (In a scared sleepy voice)

" What's going on?
What's the matter?

What are you doing?
<u>Steups</u>, You smelling of Rum..."*

DIALOGUE

MALE

" Don't you worry we's alright now
Just me and you..

We'll have our own good time right here. And right now.

You just do what I say, and everything will be just fine.."

DIRECTION

He places his hand over Mel's mouth and there is a struggle...

MALE

" Hush now.. We don't want to upset your Mummy now do we?
We do out de lite"

Then total blackout.

SCENE Ten Ends

SCENE ELEVEN Begins

SETTING: JAMES' FAMILY SITTING ROOM.
The Next Morning after the Party.

DIRECTION

The morning after the night before:

Melanie is dressed in jeans and T-shirt.
She is clearing up from the buffet table.
She is holding a plastic bag of rubbish in her left hand.

The voice of (**MOIRA / MUMMY**) is heard.

Moira pops her head around the Sitting Room Door.
Moira is dressed smartly for her days' work ahead.

MOIRA/MUMMY

DIALOGUE

" Now you make sure that all is tidy from last night, yuh hear, and
dat all is back to normal by the time I get home tonight...

And don't you forget to collect Daddy's dry cleaning later on.
The ticket there on the mantelpiece...all ready for you.

Daddy dropping Marie off to school this morning...so you don't have to
worry on dat. Anyhow it'll give you more time to clear up this mess.
See how I tink out for you?

So, you collect her and give her a bite to eat when you all come home ...
and mind you get yourself off to school on time now...

I gotta rush now, I don't want to be late!
Miranda got a busy day planned ahead for us for sure.

And we'll have much pleasantries to talk about after last night's
success I'm sure eh? It's going to be a great day!"

DIRECTION

With that Moira is on her way..
Melanie rushes to the Sitting room door to call out!

<u>DIALOGUE</u>

<u>MELANIE</u>

" But Mummy, I need money for the bus fare, I don't have any, and if
I have to walk I will be late.."

<u>DIRECTION</u>

There is no answer. The front door slams and Moira is gone.

Mel feels not only hears the door slam..
All she has said has fallen on deaf ears...Yet again.

Melanie turns back and looks around the room whilst standing in the
doorway.

There is deep silence for a while.

<u>DIALOGUE</u>

" Oh Mummy.... Mummy....
I need you .
And I need you to listen to me, just for once"

<u>DIRECTION</u>

Melanie then begins to cry softly and forlornly whilst holding a
plastic bag of rubbish.

Melanie looks at the bag and throws the plastic rubbish bag to the floor.

Melanie gathers herself enough to defiantly sing:

<u>'LIVE WITHOUT FEAR' (Full Vocal Version)</u>

<u>Scene Eleven ends / closes.</u>

<u>SCENE TWELVE Begins</u>

<u>SETTING The same Sitting Room later that day.</u>
<u>Early evening.</u>

<u>Opens with Melanie on the telephone</u>

<u>DIRECTION</u>

Melanie is talking quietly on the telephone, as if she doesn't want to be overheard.

<u>DIALOGUE</u>

<u>MELANIE</u>

" No, I'm not saying that, I just don't think I will be allowed to come.."

(Middling Pause)

" No. I've told you it's not that I don't want to, I just know they won't let me...especially her! "

(Longer Pause)

"Ok. I will try. I promise."

(Short Pause)

"Yes I'll let you know by 7pm.."

(Shorter Pause)

"Yes ok then.."

(Short Pause)

"Look, I have to go; they'll be back soon and I have to get Marie her Dinner"

(Even Shorter Pause)

"No of course I won't forget... Look I going isn't it! Before I heard!"

DIRECTION

Melanie puts down the 'phone in a bit of a panic.
She looks around, then feeling safer; she begins to wander around the
Sitting Room.
She starts to hum ('**Live Without Fear**') to herself.

A few lyrics are heard:

" She's a lone and true survivor
Going where her past won't find her
She found her strength where she thought No No No
I've had enough..."

DIRECTION

Younger Sister Marie enters the room..
Marie walks straight across to Melanie.

She immediately interrupts the singing..
Mimicking Moira / Mummy's voice she says...

DIALOGUE

MARIE

" Melanie! What is that awful caterwauling you doing?"

(Marie then goes straight into her own voice: Laughing)
Heh Mel! I scared you! I bet you thought that was Mummy! Eh?

You shouldn't be on that 'phone you know,
Mummy said you call Cherie and all..
and that that wastes lots of Daddy's money"

MELANIE

" Shut up Marie!
I never call Trinidad!

(Mel now Calms down, and uses a different tack)

Look Marie, Let's have some fun. We can both of us go into the kitchen, and you can help me get your food ready.
It'll be fun! Cookin up together.

That's what I used to do wit Grandma, all dat time ago when I was teeny, and it was always fun"

MARIE

" Mummy says I'm too young and delicate to do stuff in the kitchen.
She says it's far too dangerous; and any way when I grow up I shall have other people to do that sort of thing for me...
Because I am going to have a rich husband and be a Lady.

Not like you Mel, because you will have to fend for yourself probably.
That's what Mummy says.

Anyhow I'm going to tell Mummy that you did called Cherie.
And that I heard you talking to her! So there!"

DIRECTIONS

Marie suddenly changes tack... she is twirling her hair and herself..

"Mel, I'm hungry NOW and you gonna take ages to cook me something nice...!
All 'cos you been on that 'phone to Cherie and all.."

MELANIE (Melanie is now nervously plumping up some cushions.
She stops and turns to face Marie)

"Look, for the last time that wasn't Cherie.
In fact I didn't call anyone THEY called me.

It was a friend, here in London.
So there back!

Just mind your own business Marie.
You getting more like Mummy every day"

Melanie flops down in the comfy chair by the fireplace.. the one Moira usually sits in.
She sighs wearily as she becomes more exasperated by Marie.

MARIE

"Any ways I don't care what you say, that's what Mummy says.
(Said in a very proud voice)

And Mummy say's _you_ getting more like Daddy every day! .
Which is silly 'cos you not a boy!"

DIRECTION

(Marie begins to laugh at her own 'joke')

"Any how Mummy says you don't have any friends here..
So no one could be calling you. So there!"

MELANIE

" A lot she knows.
Well I DO, so there...
And they did call me! So double _there_ back!"

DIRECTION

Melanie stands up, drawing herself up to her full height over Marie.
Mel now speaks heavily, darkly, and slowly.

DIALOGUE

MELANIE

"Now listen Marie, you know nutten, you just a stupid little girl!
As for being like Daddy... I am nothing like him...
And never say that again...to me or anybody!

I am like ME. I am I. _Mel._
Not Melanie...Not like Daddy and certainly not like Mummy!

173

I am no – one but ME. Mel.

Yes. From now on. I am just ME!"

<u>DIRECTION</u>

Marie goes quiet and subdued for a while. She stands still looking a little scared of her sister.
Melanie's tone is not usually stern.

Mel suddenly sees Marie as the frightened little girl that she really is.
Mel puts her arm around Marie lovingly.

<u>DIALOGUE</u>

<u>MELANIE</u>

"Look, I didn't mean to scare you so Marie…
It's just well..
I don't want to be like Daddy nor like Mummy nor for you to be like dem either if the truth be told.

Look none of this is your fault Marie, so don't worry so about it all."

<u>DIRECTION</u>

<u>MELANIE</u> (Attempts to brighten up the mood.)

"Come on, let's just make your food together.
I promise you it <u>will</u> be fun.

Despite what Mummy says, you know you will need to take care of yourself just a little whether you become a lady of leisure…or not!

And hopefully one day you will be just <u>you</u> too.
Just Marie.

Not a copy of Mummy, nor anyone else come to that. Just you. Marie.

Now, what would you like to cook up?

(Mel takes Marie's hand as if she is about to lead her into the kitchen)

Let's get your dinner made before Mummy comes back."

DIRECTION

The mood having lightened.. Marie shrugs her shoulders.
Not really taking on the significance of Mel's words.
She then changes tack.

MARIE

" That's silly of course I am going to be me.
You talk silly sometimes Mel...

That's what Mummy says you do..
Talk silly.
I want my food now. (Marie stamps her foot)

And, I don't want to help in the kitchen.
I told you Mummy says it too dangerous for me in there!

And anyhow; I want to watch Television... or else I WILL tell Mummy
you were on the 'phone for HOURS!
So double double there."

DIRECTION

Melanie shakes her head whilst looking at Marie..
Mel let's go of Marie's hand.

DIALOGUE

MELANIE

" You know what Marie I give up.."

DIRECTION

Melanie looks at the clock and realises how close home time is for
Mummy / Moira.

Thus: realising she must deal with this attempted blackmail quickly,
Melanie takes a deep breath and decides to try once more to placate
Marie.
Melanie sighs. She decides to make a bargain.

<u>DIALOGUE</u>

<u>MELANIE</u>

" O.K. Marie I give in. It's getting late; there's no time for this
nonsense of yours.
Look this is the deal:

If I let you watch TV whilst you are eating, the 'phone call will be our
little secret, and you won't mention to Mummy that I was on the
'phone, at all.

O.K Do you understand?

Plus, they can tell from the bill if I 'phoned out...
So whatever you say I can prove I didn't call anyone..
That they called me..

So all of this idiocy of yours' really is a nonsense isn't it?"

<u>DIRECTION</u>

Marie looks bemused by this 'grown up' information, dismissing it as
immaterial to her cause; which is to watch TV whilst eating.
Marie just carries on with the negotiations, which she now regards as
some fun.

Marie pretends to cry (her favourite weapon of choice, which nearly
always works) and to raise her voice somewhat.

<u>DIALOGUE</u>

<u>MARIE</u>

"O.K but I want to watch NOW!
(Said to a stamp of the foot to emphasise her plea.)

So I'll _have_ to eat in here now we all late and all, not in the kitchen, if I not going to miss my favourite programme.

And so you'll have to make my dinner on your own so I can watch the Television sitting here in Mummy's best chair! So there!"

DIRECTION

Marie stamps her feet again.

MELANIE

" OK OK
You win!
Stop yelling and crying we don't want Mummy coming home to this sort of thing! Now do we?

 You know how upset she gets if you cry.. So stop it NOW!

Look! You can watch the TV here if you promise NOT to say anything to Mummy about 'phone calls AT ALL ...
And to be careful of crumbs and tings eh?
Or she'll go mad, if she find such.
That's the deal. Take it or leave it!
Now; do you promise?"

DIRECTION

Melanie takes Marie in her arms and hugs her, as Marie sobs. Mel is now feeling sorry for herself and for Marie.

Marie is now really upset as she fears Mummy might get angry with her too. There is now a silence between the two sisters.

Marie nods: Then, through sobs Marie talks:

MARIE

" Why does Mummy get so angry Mel?
 Is it because it's like she says you are bad?

That you have got the devil in you?

177

Will I get the devil in me too?
Because we are sisters?

(All this is said whilst Marie is genuinely sobbing. Also, this is the closest moment the sisters share/are seen to share)

<u>MARIE</u> (Continues)

"Mummy says I am good now and pretty but I might catch bad ways from you. Does that mean I won't stay pretty either?

Mel, were you prettier when you was young like me?
And you lost the prettiness eh?
Mel how did you catch the Devil?

Mummy, she says you have the Devil right set in you, and that's why you're not pretty.

Or is that <u>why</u> you got the Devil in you Mel?
'Cos you <u>not</u> pretty and you too dark?
How does it all work Mel? I don't really understand it all"

<u>DIRECTIONS</u>

Marie does not wait for an answer.
There is a pause, whilst Marie just thinks to herself.

Marie stops crying too quickly and abruptly.
She changes tack once again.

<u>MARIE</u> (Continues:)

"Anyhow I don't want to a Me.
I want to be like Mummy...
Cos when Mummy dies she going straight to heaven.
Because she is good.

And I want to be good like Mummy, and then I will go to heaven too!
So there. It better to be like Mummy than be like you eh Mel?"

<u>DIRECTION</u>

178

Mel just continues to hug Marie.. looking into the distance.
Marie is starting to calm down.

There is another longer silence.

<u>DIALOGUE</u>

<u>MARIE</u> (Pulls away from Mel's hold. Marie Continues)

"I don't know where Grandma went though...
Mummy says she doesn't know either.

It's all very silly.. I don't know.

Mummy doesn't get as angry with me as she does with you does she
Mel?
Not as angry as she does with you.
She does loves me though doesn't she Mel?

I get scared when Mummy is angry and unhappy, why do you make
her unhappy Mel?
Why so?"

<u>MELANIE</u>

" It's not always about me Marie. It's not always me...
Mummy has things on her mind..
Things she really doesn't understand.. Tings that trouble her bad."

<u>DIRECTION</u>

Melanie now pushes Marie further away.
Mel stares at Marie intently: looking at her silently for a moment
whilst thinking:

Then Mel speaks very strongly and sadly aloud:

<u> MELANIE TO THE AUDIENCE/ SUSPENSION</u>

"She is just a kid. It's not her fault, none of this is her fault.

NOR IS IT MINE!

We just all carrying on the pain inherited... the stories and lies put
into us from the likes of you and yours...

The centuries of lies making us all think we less...

Poor Mummy she addled with it all.

The Godliness that be put into her, the aping white ways..
She all warped and all kinds of ting like that...

She lost her real self long time.
And she threw me away in her losing."

MELANIE (To Marie) Back in Real Time/ in the now

" No Marie, Mummy doesn't get real angry with you, and yes she does
love you, and maybe she just doesn't love me, 'cos she don't know how.

So I suppose that's why she gets so angry. I don't know Marie...
And I'm now too weary to work it all out any more:

And maybe I don't need to anymore.. Not now..

But I am sure of one thing that Grandma is in a happy place for sure
Just like she always was when she was here with us.

So you don't need to worry over that none."

DIRECTION

Melanie falls silent and pensive.
She stares ahead into space.

Melanie draws in a deep breath.

DIALOGUE

MELANIE

"All you need to know is that we all love you Marie..
I just wish I could protect you more..

If only from yourself"

MARIE (Said whilst wiping her eyes, and cheering up a little)

"I'm her favourite she says so...

It's because I am so pretty and good, not like you.
Isn't it Mel?"

DIRECTION

Marie starts dancing around.
She seems to be fully recovered and to have forgotten her previous apprehensions.

DIALOGUE

MARIE

" So anyhow, I can watch TV now then?"

MELANIE (Even smiling a little)

" Yes just so long as you forget all about telephones"

MARIE

"OK!"

DIRECTION

Marie says O.K. very brightly, as if nothing has happened in the way that maybe only children can.
Melanie walks over to the TV and turns it on.

Mel leaves to go to the kitchen, whilst Marie settles down in Moira's armchair clutching a cushion, staring at the TV in the corner.

The set fades to darkness.

Scene Twelve Ends.

<u>SCENE THIRTEEN Begins.</u>

<u>Setting Back in the James' SITTING ROOM Even Later that Evening</u>

Mummy / Moira & Daddy / Michael are seated in separate armchairs.

Moira is reading a magazine, whilst Michael is surrounded by files from work. The files are spread out on his lap and onto the floor.

Melanie is sitting at the window seat gazing out across the gardens.

Marie is on the floor sitting on a cushion also reading a magazine.

Moira becomes uncomfortable in her seat; she begins to fidget.

She breaks the silence. She calls out to no one in particular at first.

<u>DIALOGUE</u>

<u>MOIRA</u>

" What in heavens name is on this chair?"

<u>DIRECTIONS</u>

Moira then directs her attention towards Melanie.
She throws down her magazine in a melodramatic fashion.

"Melanie!
What is all of this then?
What have you been doing on this chair?

Looks like there is food on here, and crumbs....
And look them all over the floor too
Lord! There are crumbs every where!

We not animals we don't eat here and on the floor..

Look I tell you there's they everywhere!..

How am I expected to sit comfortably and read in such a mess as this?
You know the rule is no food in the Sitting Room. Ever!"

DIRECTION

Michael is the first to respond to the disturbance.
He looks up from reading his papers.
The girls just look on, but they are both very apprehensive:

DIALOGUE

MICHAEL

" Calm down now Moira the children most likely had a little snack
that's all, just ease up and forget it. I will clean it up later.."

DIRECTION

Michael then deliberately turns his attention to Mel, in a bid to diffuse
the brewing situation.
Moira sighs a sulky sigh and picks up her magazine again.

DIALOGUE

DADDY/ MICHAEL

"So, how was your day Mel... (anie)?

You'll be taking those important exams at School then soon? Eh?
Are you happy with your choices and all?
We haven't had time to discuss it properly eh.
Maybe you would like to talk about it with me eh?

Before you make your final decisions.. Maybe I could help out a little.
I done it all myself you know..
But that was a long time ago now eh?"

DIRECTION

Melanie turns to face her Father wearily.
She answers in a monotone voice.

DIALOGUE

MELANIE

" My day was fine Daddy.. Just fine.

And yes, I'm happy enough with my choices.
We don't need to talk, not really"

MICHAEL/ DADDY

" So what you decided you taking then?
Happy enough doesn't sound too convincing to me, does it to you
Mummy?"

DIRECTIONS

Michael puts down his files and papers in order to give Melanie his full attention.
Moira on the other hand could not be less interested.
She still continues to read her magazine and to fidget over the crumbs in her chair.

Marie follows suit, (because Mummy seems calm again)

MICHAEL continues:

"It is important you know.
Very important.
Your choices and all will determine your entire future you know!

I would like you to go to University like I did...
That's what makes you get on, stand out from the crowd and all."

DIRECTION

Mel has now turned fully away from the window and her day dreaming..
She too is now focussed properly upon the conversation with her Father.

MICHAEL (Continues:)

"You could have a bright future if you do well and all.
So your choices are vital to success you know.
I should know.

I would be just another black man driving a bus or something without my degree...
Nothing wrong with driving a bus you know..
But not much money in it eh?
(He laff)
And it must get tedious eh? Round and round all day!

It would drive <u>me</u> crazy..
You don't want to be getting no job that drive you crazy eh?"

DIRECTION

At this change of subject, Moira stops fidgeting and lets' go of the crumbs complaint. She is sensing she could have more sport with this conversation.

She turns her attention onto Michael. In order to bring the spotlight now to herself, and thus away from Mel.

MUMMY/ MOIRA

" What's all this about Daddy?

You filling her head with things that are not for girls and certainly not for girls like Melanie.

There's no point in such.

She's a girl and you had better get used to it Daddy..
You always trying to punish me for not giving you a son.
Don't you know how that hurts me so?"

DIRECTION

<u>MOIRA</u> (As she begins to feign a little sob) She continues:

"What she needs is to learn how to be a good Wife and Mother first.

Not all this fancy talk about University.
Melanie not clever enough for that any how"

DADDY / MICHAEL

" What do you mean? Like you?
You not exactly the maternal type when it comes down to it Moira..."

DIRECTION

Moira glowers at the use of her name in front of the girls:
Michael immediately corrects himself...
But nevertheless continues his point forcefully:

MICHAEL

"I mean Mummy...

You go out to work and all. And you enjoy doing so!
You get satisfaction from it! And wit your own money and such like.

I don't see you tied to no kitchen sink and all eh?

The girl got a brain, she need to use it!

She don't want to be no skivy.
So leave this to me and her.
It's she life ...and all after all eh!

Anyway's it's our duty to do what is best for her, and for her future...
Whatever it might be.

She need to fulfil her potential you know
Every one <u>need</u> that.
I thought you about women's rights and all sorts of ting like that?

Or it only for you eh?"

DIRECTION

Michael rises up to his full height.
Is Michael finally standing up to Moira? Literally and >

He bends down to loom over Moira in her chair.
For a fleeting moment he seems threatening..

DIALOGUE

DADDY/MICHAEL

" And what's more Woman,
I have NEVER said anything to you about not having a son.

It is all in YOUR head!

I love my Girls.. and I want the best for them.
And I mean BOTH of them!
To have choices and such like!

So now tell me, just what is your problem with that eh?"

DIRECTION

Michael steps back realising he has maybe overstepped the mark a
little, and that he may have frightened his female family.
They all three look taken aback and somewhat startled.
They all three are silent and not moving at all.

He has never spoken like this before.. in a strident manner...
so the three <u>are</u> genuinely shocked.

Michael takes a deep breath.. and steps back from Moira.
Michael walks over to his chair again, he picks up a few papers.. and
pretends to shuffle them somewhat in his hands; as if he is finished
talking, and wants to bring things to an end.

Michael looks a bit embarrassed, and slightly regretful.

Moira now gets up from the chair in a flustered manner.

She too is now on the back foot.
But true to form only momentarily.

As Marie had done earlier in the day Moira wipes out the last few
moments from her mind, and collects herself.
She straightens down her dress nervously.

She is immediately transformed to her usual self.

Moira takes control again as Marie gets up and runs to her Mother with tears in her eyes.
Marie is frightened and visibly upset, and immediately takes hold of Mummy around her waist. This 'frank' discussion is not usual in the family.

Moira allows her to hold on for a short time, then pulls her off.

DIALOGUE

MOIRA/MUMMY

" Daddy dear, now don't upset yourself so.
(Now walking across to Michael)

I just mean most men prefer a son and all, at least one.

That's all I mean, and Melanie, well it might be too much for her.
You know all that studying.. and your expectations and all.

Too much pressure for a girl and all kinds of thing like that."

DIRECTION

Moira places her hand upon Michael's shoulder, patting him.

MOIRA/ MUMMY

"Anyway now, she dun told me she just wants to get married and all.
Didn't you Melanie?
You know? When we have those Mother and Daughter chats.

She wouldn't tell you that Daddy.
She wouldn't want to upset you...to worry you out and such.
She doesn't want to feel she letting you down at all.
And she doesn't want you wasting your hard earned money when she not up to it!

Isn't that what you said Melanie dear?
Sometimes Melanie can be a thoughtful daughter...

You know how she likes to please you."

188

<u>MICHAEL</u> (Turning in shock towards Melanie)

"Mel is this true?
Tell me Mel. Is it true what your Mummy says?"

<u>MOIRA</u> (Interrupts before Melanie can answer)

" She knows what you are like about learning and all kinds of things
like that.
And she not sure she up to it at all.
Are you Melanie dear?
Tell your Daddy Melanie! Don't take fright so...

Any how's daughters need money for a proper wedding and all kinds
of ting like that eh?
They have such dreams Daddy, they have such dreams"

<u>DIRECTION</u>

Marie tries to cling to her Mummy again.
But Moira is having none of it. She pushes her away.

<u>MOIRA / MUMMY</u>

" Go back to your reading...Marie...This all don't concern you.

See Daddy? she reading about wedding dresses and such..
See what girls' dream of Daddy? ... See what they really dream of fuh
sure!"

<u>DIRECTIONS</u>

Marie dutifully goes back to reading her magazine in her previous
position of sitting on a cushion on the floor:

Melanie looks up as if she is praying for release, which may never
come. Mel remains silent.

All is frozen:

<u>MELANIE TO THE AUDIENCE/ SUSPENSION</u>

" I have told myself I will stop lying to protect everyone..

I will tell the truth.. Stand up to her, to him.
Be there for Me! "

DIRECTION
Back to Real Time in the now:

DIALOGUE

MELANIE
(Blurted out forcefully, like a pressure cooker releasing steam)

" No! It's not true..."

DIRECTION

Before Mel can continue simultaneously Marie shouts out over Mel:
Maybe she too is somehow looking to diffuse the situation somehow,
and this is all she can think to do.
Marie stands up and blurts out:

DIALOGUE

MARIE

" Melanie told me sit in your chair Mummy, when you out:

She said to watch TV and she said to eat when I watching Mummy, to
save time, because she was late in cooking for me.

She wanted me to be finished before you came home..
So you wouldn't know she all late and such.
That's why the food is there Mummy... and all those crumbs.

I do think I caught the Devil from Melanie!"

DIRECTION

MARIE (Continues between sobs:)

"She said I should do it so I wouldn't talk about telephones.

190

Melanie telephoned Cherie! (Blurted out!)

She did Mummy! That why she so late and all..

She was talking to her for a long time Mummy..
So it will cost a lot of Daddy's hard earned money!

And she talked to her other friends!

And she said to her friend that bad things happened to her that she
keeps secret..

She did Mummy. I heard her!

She does have friends in London Mummy she does..."

DIRECTION

Now, there is an even bigger stunned SILENCE all round.
Marie starts to sob again:

Everyone reverts back to type.
The Status Quo is completed. Everything has come full circle.
Moira is reigning again.

Marie runs over to Moira / Mummy.

Moira pushes Marie to one side.

DIALOGUE

MOIRA/MUMMY

" Don't cling so child!
Daddy. Please take Marie to the bathroom, and get her ready for bed.

(Said whilst Turning to Marie)
Off you go now Marie wit Daddy, you have school in the morning
child... "

MARIE

" You not angry with me Mummy are you?
You still love me don't you Mummy?"

MOIRA / MUMMY

"Of course I'm not angry with you child, you still my pretty lovely child."

DIRECTION

Moira goes over and kisses Marie hastily and insincerely.
Almost as a display to Michael of her maternal feelings towards Marie.

MOIRA (Continues)

"Now go along with Daddy and get your beauty sleep.
You see how it works!
And forget about Melanie.. she talk ole talk and lie such"

DADDY/MICHAEL (Said in a shaky voice)

" Melanie! What is this you saying?"

MOIRA/MUMMY (Said harshly even triumphantly)

" Leave this to me Daddy this is my work..
This is woman's work and that is no lie!"

DIRECTION

All else is now forgotten.
Michael/ Daddy sheepishly takes Marie by the hand and leads her off.
His head is down, in defeat, confusion and sadness.

The two women are left facing one another, staring angrily.

Fades away into darkness

LONG PAUSE > > >

DIRECTIONS

Opens with The two Women facing one another as we left them.
As if frozen in time.
The dialogue begins quietly almost in a whisper.

They turn from one another to face the audience.
They speak alternatively, directing the remarks out into the
auditorium.
It all builds up slowly to a crescendo:

DIALOGUE

MOIRA/MUMMY	MELANIE
" Yuh Jamette. You whore.	"It wasn't my fault.
You bin told you must keep this to yourself.	He made me.
No decent man will marry you now.	You know him.
You can't hope for a white man now.	WHAT!
Don't tell your Daddy.	But MUMMY!
You LIAR.	I HATE YOU!
You damaged goods now fuh true!"	I not a ting!"

DIRECTION
There is SILENCE for some time.

"You must have led him on.	"I was asleep; I didn't know what...He keep on...
If it known, the shame will break this family up.	What about ME!

They will think we are animals!"

Why don't you love me Mummy?"

DIRECTION

The following is almost said whilst talking over one another:

MOIRA/MUMMY   MELANIE

" You SO BLACK:
You SOO ugly and all!
What hope of de Wedding and all dat now eh?"

"Wedding?
What wedding you
talk of? Who care
about all dat
stupidness?"

DIRECTION

They both weep.
Silence Again. As if frozen in Time.

MUMMY/ MOIRA stands with her head bowed in PRAYER.

DIALOGUE

MOIRA

" Oh My Lord!
What am I to do? What am I to Do?"

DIRECTION

Then MOIRA gets on her knees.
She stays there throughout the song, silently praying.

MELANIE turns to the audience and SINGS

'EVERYDAY IS LIKE AN OPERA' (Full Vocal Version)

Scene Thirteen Ends

SCENE FOURTEEN Begins

SETTING OPENS IN Young PERSONS' DANCE HALL. LONDON.

DIRECTIONS

Opens in 'cute ' modest Dance Hall . It is maybe a church hall?

Lots of younger people mill about talking, drinking soft drinks from
bottles with straws. No alcohol is available.

They are all dressed to impress.
It is a typical London cosmopolitan crowd.

Some are sitting around white covered tables.
Others are dancing to:

'Just Go' Disco Instrumental version. (Played by Silent DJ)

Melanie is surrounded by the older girls seen previously in the
schoolyard.
There is general melee and noise from chattering & music etc.

Carrie, Betsy & Joanie are standing closest to Melanie.
They are now a unit of friends.
They are now easy and familiar with one another.

They are also drinking soft drinks from bottles with straws.
They are listening and reacting to the music; laughing and talking
excitedly.

DIALOGUE

CARRIE

"So how come your old man let you come out tonight Mel?
He get one over on your Mum at last then eh?

I thought it sounded like she would never let you out alone in this big
bad city of ours eh?"

DIRECTION

Melanie looks sheepish as if she doesn't want to get drawn into another debate with Carrie, especially about this evenings' outing.

This is Melanie's first big night out as a ' grown up' alone.
Melanie speaks in what she hopes is a matter of fact way.

<u>MELANIE</u>

" Oh, That's all sorted out, from now on I can do whatever I like."

<u>CARRIE</u>

<u>DIRECTION</u>

Carrie sidles up to Mel. She dances around Mel in a teasing manner.
Carrie talks close up into Mel's face...

The following is said in an attempt to <u>mimic Mel</u>..
and to tease her in a patronising fashion. Carrie repeats Mel's words:

<u>CARRIE</u>

" Oh that's all sorted out, from now on I can do whatever I like...

(Carrie continues in her '**own**' voice:)

Sooooo... that means you can get yourself a boyfriend now...eh?

I mean, you do know how to do that don't you Mel?
You being so grown up now and all"

<u>MELANIE</u>

" Of Course I do..!"

<u>DIRECTION</u>

This is said in a bid to be defiant.
However it doesn't quite work.. as Melanie is on unsure ground, she therefore sounds slightly panicky.

<u>CARRIE</u> (Said as before <u>mimicking Mel's voice</u>)

196

" Of course I do!

DIRECTION (Now, said in **Carries' own voice**, whilst
again dancing around Mel in a slightly intimidating fashion;)

All right then show us how.
How do you get yourself a boyfriend eh Mel?

I mean tonight at this dance!

Show us how **you** get yourself a boyfriend then Mel?

Heh you all, I present Mel the femme fatale eh?"

DIRECTION

The last line is said to the other girls in the group.
Carrie is laughing now at her own challenge.

Carrie though now a 'friend' of Mel's still harbours some resentment
towards Mel, maybe a little wary of Mel's attributes?
(Such as her looks and talents)

Carrie turns around to everyone in an attempt to gather support in her
teasing of Melanie.

Melanie draws herself up to her tallest, and finds her defiant voice: in
order to 'fight' back:

MELANIE

" Ok Then I WILL!

I'll show you, I'll show you Miss Carrie know it all..
Any way now, I don't see no boyfriend of yours around at any time."

DIRECTION

The music strikes up. **IT'S ALL FOR LOVE**
The Girls all react excitedly and move aside rushing over to the bar to
put their drinks down, so that they might dance unimpeded.

197

Melanie is the first to rush over to the centre of the Dance Hall just as the music begins to get going.

<u>DIALOGUE</u>

<u>MELANIE</u>

" Heh come on join in! Let's dance..

 I love this song.. Let's all do the moves...I'll show you how"

<u>DIRECTION</u>

The girls all rush across to join Mel. The song is:

<u>'IT'S ALL FOR LOVE' (Full VOCAL Version) Sung by Melanie</u>

This song is played as at a Disco.
The other girls are soon able to pick up and copy Melanie's moves.

They begin the **<u>SET DANCE ROUTINE></u>**

 <u>DIRECTION. Note: RANDOM BOY</u> sings the deep male voice part.

The girls begin to gather an increasing of audience / participants around them. Soon some of them join in with the girls.

Later into the song Mel's friends also sing along.

At end of the song Melanie and her girls fall into a heap of laughter and friendship.

Eventually as the song ends; some potential boy suitors appear at their sides.

<u>DIALOGUE</u>

<u>RANDOM BOY</u>

(Said to no one in particular...
That is to any girl who might be interested!)

" Heh.. How you girls doing! That was thirsty work!
You all fancy a Cola or what?"

<u>DIRECTION</u> (continued)

The girls all start to giggle shyly, and excitedly.
They move off with the boys loosely at first...
Then they all naturally begin to pair off.
But Mel stays put; alone.

As the others leave, Mel finds herself alone centre stage, with one boy
in particular to her side, who has stayed behind too.

They are now alone together, as the crowd melts/ fades into the
background.
The scene around the two softens to concentrate upon them solely.

The young man (Simon) starts to talk with Mel.

There is **<u>Background Instrumental beat</u>** being played again, from:

<u>It's All For Love.</u> Muted fading chatter can also be heard.

Dancing continues a little then the background fades even more.

Time stands still.

<u>**Everyone and all else fades into a suspended blurred background, as**</u>

We focus completely upon <u>MELANIE</u> and her first meeting with
<u>SIMON</u>. (There continues a background beat)

<u>DIRECTION</u> Simon speaks easily and confidently.

<u>DIALOGUE</u>

<u>SIMON</u>

" Heh... you dance beautifully. So naturally.
I'm pretty hopeless!

I can see how at home you are with music...

Do you play an instrument?"

DIRECTION
These (Mel's) words are spoken shyly, quietly and hesitantly.

MELANIE

" Erh... No. I just sing a little.
But I would love to learn... I've just not had the chance ..."

SIMON

"Would you care to sit down... over there?
We could chat a while"

DIRECTION

Simon points to an empty table in the corner.
Mel nods in shy agreement.
They walk across to a table to sit down.
Simon continues:

SIMON

" So, what would you like to play? If you had the opportunity?"

MELANIE
(Now starting to feel more at ease, Mel feels able to open up a little.)

"Oh Piano!"(Said excitedly)

(Pause)

"I would love to learn Piano. (Said more reticently)
I think it would help me..."

DIRECTION.

Mel stops abruptly:
Simon senses Mel's shyness. He speaks in an even more gentle tone.

SIMON

" Don't be shy..
Say it out loud..
What would it help you with?"

DIRECTION

After an awkward silence...Mel looks around in a lost manner.
Mel finally gains the courage to speak up.

MELANIE

" Well. I know it sounds silly.. But I write songs.

Just in my head..
And I think it would be nice to play them.. to hear them out loud to myself... not just with my voice.

Although I do sing them.. out loud I mean;
But mainly only to myself though.....as I make them up.

But it's all there the words, the music, the arrangements... everything in my head.
I can hear them, instruments and all: just how they are meant to be!"

DIRECTION

Melanie becomes a little more confident, animated and excited.

MELANIE Continues:

"So, though I can hear it all in my head...
I just can't play it out into the world, properly.
It can be a bit frustrating, it not going nowhere else!

Well, not yet anyhow... (Mel laughs a little)

But if I learnt Piano...Well that would be a start..
It would be lovely.
Like the conversation would be complete some how!"

DIRECTION

Mel's voice trails off...
Her voice becomes quieter fearing she has opened up too much too soon.
And to a stranger! Mel looks over towards her friends, thinking she
might make excuses to leave, and go over to them. Though in the
blurred background they seem able to tune in to watch her every move.

Simon has been listening carefully with an admiring smile on his
face. There is an awkward pause (For Mel)

Finally Mel looks back at Simon, she continues:

<u>MELANIE</u>

"Does that sound mad to you?

Mummy says it is.."

Melanie's voice drifts off again and she stops talking altogether.
This time she gazes down at nothing in particular on the table:
Now thinking she really <u>has</u> gone too far:

<u>**DIRECTION There is another silence.**</u>

Simon looks intently at Mel.
Eventually he speaks..

<u>SIMON</u>

"No it doesn't...
Sound mad I mean.
Far from it.

So, what's your name?"

<u>MELANIE</u>   (Looking up, with a little more confidence, and some
relief: Thinking: Heh he doesn't think I am mad!)

"It's Melanie..
But I like to be called Mel.."

<u>SIMON</u>

"Well it's very nice to meet you... Melanie, who likes to be called Mel. I'm Simon."

DIRECTION

Simon reaches across the table and takes Mel's hand in his, with his other hand placed over the top of Mel's.
He shakes it very gently and slowly, whilst all the time gazing into Mel's eyes.
Something, a connection, is very clearly happening between them.

DIALOGUE

SIMON

"Well Melanie... Who likes to be called Mel,

All I can do is; confirm that is it is not mad to hear music in your head.

All the great composers heard music in their heads...

How do you think it all got out onto the page and onto the piano, and all the other instruments?

It's just great that you can do that...

I wish I could do it.

Not only can I not dance very well, but also I cannot compose music much either.
Well nothing anyone would care to listen to that is.

I have all the theory but no writing talent whatsoever!"

DIRECTION
Simon begins to laugh to himself.

" I can play but... that's it.

Never written a song in my life...
Apart from some stuff for exams.

But really nothing of any note that is.

It's funny isn't it?

How 'talents' seem to choose you. Not you them!
Just like love I guess........"

<u>MELANIE</u> (Now getting a bit flustered)

" When you put it like that... I guess so.

I mean it isn't mad after all...

As for love... I wouldn't know about it."

<u>DIRECTIONS</u>

Both Simon and Mel laugh a little together.
The ice is broken. Any tensions relieved.

At this point Simons' friends are gesturing to him to go.
They wave at him to come over to them.

He responds to them, and calls out:

<u>SIMON</u>

" O.K I'm coming... just a minute!"

<u>DIRECTION</u>

Simon faces Mel, and reaching into his pocket he hands her a card.
Simon places the card onto the table in a deliberate fashion:

Mel takes the card and looks at it. Then holds it to her.

<u>SIMON</u>

" That's my lift home from my friends...We all came in the one car.
I can't keep them waiting.
However much I would like to stay! I must go.
Look Mel, my 'phone number's on that card.

It would be great to see you again…

Maybe go out to lunch and get to know one another better.
Continue this conversation a little.
What do you think?

Give me a call if you would like to..
I know I would… like to.
Very much."

MELANIE (Said softly)

" I think I would like to too. That would be lovely…"

DIRECTION

Simon stands up as does Mel.

They are both beaming shyly.

DIALOGUE

SIMON

" Great, That's just great..

So I'll see you soon…?"

DIRECTION

Simon turns to go… hesitates and looks back to Mel. He calls out:

SIMON

"Don't lose the card will you?"

MELANIE

" No, No, I won't lose it."

DIRECTION

Simons' friends call out to him again. Meanwhile Carrie, Betsy and Joanie have wandered across ' **back into the now'** to witness the scene.

Simon stops and turns back to give Mel a quick chaste kiss on the cheek.

Simon runs across to join his friends, and turns to wave goodnight to Mel one last time.

Mel waves back with the hand that is holding Simons' card.
Simon and his friends leave.

Mel watches them go, and eventually realises she has the card in her hand.
Mel looks at it, and then gives the card a brief peck.

At this point the three friends gather around Mel excitedly.

CARRIE

" Oh My God!
 She's only gone and done it..

Mel. I never thought you had it in you.."

BETSY

" Well I did.."

JOANIE

" Me too..
And he seems really nice..."

BETSY

" Yeah the kind you can take home to Mother!"

DIRECTION

Melanie's face drops as if the reality of what may happen has come to her..

CARRIE

" Well maybe not your Mother...not the way she is.
But at least she'll be pleased that he's wh "...

BETSY & JOANIE (In Unison cut Carrie off in full flow)

"Carrie shut up!"

BETSY (Putting her arm around Mel)

"Don't mind her Mel..
The brain doesn't always engage with her mouth."

JOANIE

"In fact I think it never does!"

DIRECTION

Mel looks a little crestfallen.
Carrie for once looks embarrassed.
She looks down at her feet

DIALOGUE

CARRIE

" I didn't mean nothing by it Mel..
I didn't mean to upset the moment for you.

I just meant your Mum would be glad he was ..
You know; what she wants for you"

BETSY

" You know what Caz I really do think you have a serious foot in
mouth problem!"

207

CARRIE

" Look I'm just trying to explain to Mel I never meant nothing I swear! You get me don't you Mel?"

DIRECTION

With that Joanie decides to diffuse the situation, before things start to become heated.

JOANIE

" You know what I think ?

I think we should get our coats before they close the cloakroom.

And what's more I think if we don't move now we will miss our bus...

And if we miss our bus! We'll ALL be for it.

As things going even if we do make it home we so late we'll have a hell of a job ever getting out again!"

(Joanie puts her arm around Mel again...)

JOANIE

" Come on Mel.. She don't really mean anything you know...
Let's not spoil the night...
Let's go home..."

CARRIE

"Yeah .. we've had a great night..
The Four Brits hitting the town eh!"

JOANIE

"Yeah. We'll be out on the town again next week eh?
Well hopefully, if we ever get home tonight eh?
Girls never to be parted."

DIRECTION

Mel now puts her arms around all three girls. They have a group hug to cement their friendships. Mel is smiling again.

MELANIE

" You bet... London Girls Forever!

You all go ahead and get the coats..

I'll just catch up with my thoughts, maybe work out what I'm going to say to Mummy!
I'll meet you all in the foyer in a bit"

CARRIE & BETSY

" O.K Mel .. See you in a sec.."

JOANIE

" You O.K now Mel?"

MELANIE (Dreamily)

" Yes, Joanie.. I am..
In fact for once I think I am more than OK...!"

DIRECTION

With that the three girls leave the Hall to go to collect their coats.

Melanie stands alone holding Simons' card close to her.

The set now has lowered lighting..
The Dance Hall set behind gradually becomes faded, darker and quieter.

New music begins. (ALL YOU WANT FROM ME)

Two figures emerge in order to dance a smoochy Dream like dance to the song behind Melanie as she sings:

<u>MELANIE SINGS></u>

<u>'ALL YOU WANT FROM ME'</u> (Full vocal version)

This is Melanie imagining how things could turn out for her and Simon.

<u>CLOSE SCENE Fourteen</u>

SETTING

Opens with Marquee set up in a Suburban Garden in London.

The Marquee is set out with a high table at one end, together with other round white covered tables with chairs all around.

The debris of food and drinks can be seen everywhere.

There is small stage set up to the side with speakers and sound equipment set up together with some musicians and a female Singer. To the side of that there is a small set up for a DJ.

Melanie & Cherie are standing to one side watching the action: As are Michael & Moira.

Simon with his best man are standing with drinks in hand on the other side. They are animated carefree and laughing.

The band are playing the Song 'TICK TOCK' FULL Vocal Version. Some stalwart guests are still dancing in the centre of the Marquee.

DIRECTION

At the end of the song The Singer takes the applause and thanks the crowd. She says:

FEMALE SINGER with the Band

" That's us for TONIGHT!

I hope you all had a great time, I know we did!

Let's have one more hand for the Happy Couple and a Bon Voyage from all of us..
Good night...Thanks. Thank you!"

DIRECTION

The singer claps her hands, as does the band for the couple.

Simon and Mel bow in acknowledgement.
A bit more applause comes from the few guests who were dancing.

The guests' retreat to the side tables in a somewhat bedraggled state,
finally ready to end the evening.
There is the distinct air of winding down.

The Singer sits down on the edge of the stage.

She begins to put her music and belongings into her bags.
The musicians fiddle about with their instruments and dismantling
some kit.

They are chatting amongst themselves.

Female SINGER with the Band. (Is heard to say:)

" It was a good night guys, yeah, a nice little earner.
They make a cute couple too…"

There continues a general hum of indiscernible chatter amongst the
few remaining guests.
 A few people remain at tables, whilst others are starting to drift away..

It is a typical appearance of the end of a Wedding Reception.

Mummy and Daddy are still standing to one side quietly surveying
the scene.

DIALOGUE TO THE AUDIENCE / SUSPENSION

MOIRA/MUMMY

" Well you all, I never thought our Melanie would do it you know!
Thank the Lord ! What a weight from my shoulders.
No more worries for me on that score eh?
The Lord he does move in mysterious ways fuh true.

I'll get those light Grans' now for sure.

But Marie's will be better prospects when her time comes.
You know that Melanie!

212

She sooo dark and all that..

Though he is soo light..."

DIRECTION

(Said thoughtfully whilst staring across at/ towards Simon)

Thank the Lord
(Said with a nod towards The Lord above)

We'll have to wait and see how things turn out fuh true...eh?

It better than I ever hoped for anyhow eh?
Makes up a bit for having to put up with...

Anywise never mind on all that now eh?"

DIRECTION

Moira and Michael walk away **IN REAL Time / The Now.**
Leaving Melanie alone with her best friend CHERIE.
The focus is now upon the two best friends.

Melanie is holding hands with **CHERIE** who has come over from
Trinidad for the Wedding.

The band continue to clear up, and relax.

Someone takes drinks over to them, which they start to drink up
gratefully.

DIALOGUE

MELANIE

" Cherie I am so glad you were able to come over...

I have missed you so much.

Your being here has made this day even more perfect...

You know you've always been like a sister to me don't you?

I couldn't imagine today without you being here!"

CHERIE

" I've always felt the same about you Mel! I have so missed you.
Like there was a part of my family gone.

I couldn't believe it when our Daddy's said they would club together
and pay for my trip; I was so excited. And if the truth be told a little
scared of the trip and all.
But, it's been so worth it... it really has been..."

DIRECTION

At this point Cherie seems at a loss for words;
She begins to twirl around with happiness in order to regain her
momentum. She sighs a contented sigh.

DIALOGUE

CHERIE

" You know what Mel?
It has been what I call; a Wonderful Day!

That's what it's been...

Just a Wonderful, Wonderful Day!"

DIRECTION

Music now emanates from the DJ's CD player from over by the far
stage.

Mel begins to sing: Cherie continues to dance around Mel whilst

MELANIE

Is Singing:

'IT'S A WONDERFUL DAY' (Full Vocal Version)

214

At the end of the song Cherie claps and the girls fall into each other's arms.

CHERIE

DIALOGUE

' Mel, that was beautiful.
You are so talented Mel... You have such a lovely voice.
Don't ever forget it will you?
Don't let go of your dreams, your music..."

DIRECTION

The two women hug again.

CHERIE

"At times I thought I was never going to see you ever again...
Today has truly been a wonderful day for everybody and that song...
Well it's ... it just describes everything perfectly.
I am so happy for you...For you both. (Looking across to Simon)

In fact I'm even happy for those two!"
(Said whilst turning her head towards Moira & Michael)

DIRECTIONS

Mel's Mummy & Daddy have returned.

They sit down at a table again with a last drink of the evening:
They are chatting to one another quietly.

Both the girls look over towards them.
Mel laughs out very loudly.

MELANIE

" Yes. I suppose so. Even for those two.
But especially for me Cherie...because

I'm free of them now forever.

I just wish..."

<u>DIRECTION</u>

Suddenly Mel looks sad. She is quiet for a time.

<u>MELANIE</u>

" Oh you know. "

<u>CHERIE</u>

" I know Mel, but we can't have everything, and she will be looking
down on you.
You know that for sure"

<u>MELANIE</u>

" You think so Cherie?
I guess if anyone is able to Grandma will do it."

<u>CHERIE</u>

" You bet!
She was here this whole Wonderful Day! I'd say for sure !"

<u>DIRECTION</u>

From across the Marquee SIMON comes striding over..
He takes Mel in his arms and whisks her around. They are so happy.

<u>SIMON</u>

" Darling Mel it's time to go, time to say the rest of your farewells..."

<u>DIRECTION</u>

Simon turns his attention to Cherie..

<u>DIALOGUE</u>

<u>SIMON</u>

" It was great meeting you Cherie...
We'll meet up again when we come home.
You'll still be here when we get back?"

CHERIE

" Gosh I hope so.
Look I have some news. In fact I'm going to see if I can get onto a
college course here. So you might be stuck with me for some time yet"

SIMON

"That's great news. Good for you!
It'll be so good for Mel to have her other sister around 'fuh true'"

(The last two words are said in an attempt at Trini lingo)

MELANIE (Said very excitedly)

" Cherie! Why didn't you say so before?"

CHERIE

" Well we haven't exactly had much time to talk..
And...Well, you have been kind of busy with other things!

(They all exchange bashful smiles)

"And anyhow nothing is settled yet; and I didn't want to get up your
hopes too high .. Nor mine for that matter!
Just in case nothing comes of it."

MELANIE

" Don't worry Daddy is good at things like that... he will steer you in
the right direction..
It really is the best news ever... and today of all days too!"

DIRECTION

Mel turns to Simon

<u>DIALOGUE</u>

<u>MELANIE</u>

" Oh, Simon can't we have just one more dance?
The band's still here.
Just one more!

Some how I don't want this part of the day to end... not just yet"

<u>DIRECTION</u>

Mel looks all around.
Then her gaze settles on the band, which are still packing up.
The singer is just about to leave.
The marquee is almost empty by now.

Melanie runs across to ask them to play one more tune.
Mel places her hand onto the Singers' shoulder:
Simon & Cherie look on lovingly with amusement.

<u>DIALOGUE</u>

<u>MELANIE</u>

"Please don't go just yet!
 Can you play this one for us?
For just one last dance..

I know you're all tired, but it would mean so much to me,
(Mel turns her head around to look at Simon)
To us"

<u>DIRECTION</u>

Mel gently guides The Singer over to the edge of the stage and hands
her some song sheets she had secreted at the side of the stage
previously....
The Singer briefly looks through the music...

<u>DIALOGUE</u>

Female SINGER with the Band

"Go on then. O.K Darlin' just for you... But just this one mind you.
(Turning to the band)
All right boys take a look at this. Mmm."

DIRECTION

The band stops what they were doing to look up.
The Singer hands around the song sheets...
The Band all gather around to scan through the music together...
The Band unpack somewhat, and start to prepare:
They get into their positions, and start to tune up.
Then have quick run through.

Meanwhile Mel runs back across to Simon and Cherie.

DIALOGUE
SIMON

"I do believe you had this planned! You minx!
Is it one of your songs?
The one you've been working on by any chance?"

MELANIE (Said in a playful, almost coquettish manner)

" It might be! You'll find out soon enough"

DIRECTION

The Band begins to play properly.
Simon takes Mel into his arms, lovingly romantically.

They begin to dance.
Cherie looks on happily..

'BEFORE WE MET' (Full Vocal Version) Sung by
The Female Singer with the Band from the stage.

DIRECTION

Three quarters of the way through the song Simon waves to Cherie to
join them..
She shyly goes across, and they end the dance together as a trio.
As the music fades the three hug one another in friendship.
Meanwhile; Mummy and Daddy get up and start to walk off stage.
Mummy / MOIRA turns to Daddy MICHAEL.

DIALOGUE

MOIRA

" We lost her now for sure... Though I never thought she would get.."

MICHAEL (Said angrily)

" Now you just ease up yuh mouth now Moira!

I don't want to hear no more of that talk..
Not today, and not ever again..

Go and find YOUR child...

We lost her!
You lost her long time. You threw her away.

But she always be my daughter, whatever,
She my little girl"

DIRECTION

The pair wander off together without looking back.
Michael waves without turning around.

A Life Chapter is OVER.

End of Scene Fifteen

END OF PART/ACT ONE

220

PART/ACT TWO Begins

SCENE SIXTEEN Begins

SETTING. A few months later.

Set in Simon & Melanie's Flat, in London.
They are in their bedroom.

DIRECTION

Opens with Melanie sitting on the side of the Marital Bed.

She is dressed in a pretty linen floral summer dress.
Strewn over the bed are magazines.
There is a photo of Simon & Mel together on the dresser.

Simon walks into the room. He is adjusting his shirt collar.

DIALOGUE

SIMON

" Are you ready yet Mel?
 We have to be there by two thirty you know.
 I don't want to be late.
 I have to make, I mean we have to make a good impression."

Melanie looks up and sighs, and stretches.

MELANIE

"Mm. I'm almost ready, I just have to find the right shoes and I'm
done. Will there be many people there?"

SIMON

" Should be, you know what these things are like, the boss invites and
everyone says yes, what a great idea. A bit like a royal command, or
volunteering in the army... they say jump and you say how high."

They both laugh and Simon falls onto the bed next to Melanie...
They are very relaxed and in love with one another.

Simon picks up one of the magazines (that Mel has been reading)
and nonchalantly begins to flick through some pages..

Simon notices Mel has been reading an article on pregnancy and
Motherhood.

DIALOGUE

SIMON

" So what's all this then? Babies!
Is there something you haven't told me?" (Said with light humour)

MELANIE (Laughs)

"NO! I just looking, acquainting myself with some facts!

They always look so cute, and, we have said one day...
I know it will be a while yet, but one day."

DIRECTIONS

Melanie looks dreamily once again at the magazine pictures.

DIALOGUE

SIMON

" Absolutely.. AND we shall one day. We'll have at least two!"

MELANIE

" Everybody has two... _We_ should have three!"

DIRECTION

Simon sits up excitedly!

DIALOGUE

SIMON

"No four, we shall have four, I like even numbers, and that way no-one feels left out.
They will always have some one to play with."

MELANIE

"Well it's not going to happen in this flat!
Mmm. Hang on a minute!
I think I've changed my mind, you don't have to have them I do!
So on second thoughts! I think two will do very nicely after all"

DIRECTION

They both giggle.. Simon leans back on the pillows with his hands behind his head.

SIMON

" Yes, Maybe you're right, and seeing as to how I have to pay for them, maybe we should stop at two!

But Mel, we won't be in this flat forever you know.
In fact, maybe not for much longer.

If today goes well.. Promotion may be on the cards and then we will be able to save faster for a house..

Which means... with your consent Madam...
We could accommodate a football team."

MELANIE

" Now you _are_ joking, you can do _that_ dream on your own for sure!"

DIRECTION

They both stand up, holding hands and laughing.
Simon starts to light heartedly tickle Mel. The banter continues.

MELANIE

"And what's this about you having to pay for them?
I bring in enough to pay for them myself too"

SIMON

" I know. But, well....
They will need their Mum at home. At least when they are small.

Remember how you hated being alone as a child when your Mum
wasn't around?"

MELANIE

" That was different..
It wasn't her I was missing far from it.
Though I did have Grandma around for me, I have to admit.
But, I was glad it wasn't Mummy around.

I do know what you mean though...
Kids need someone they can rely on to be there for them.

It's all so difficult.. to do the right thing I mean..

(Thoughtful pause, and sigh...)

Anyhow...we will manage together.... We'll sort it out between us.

One on duty then the other! You'll make a great Dad.
Even though you do have some very old fashioned views young Simon,
that's all I can say"

SIMON

" And you'll make a wonderful Mum! Kind, sweet Mel.
So I will bow to your Feminist sensitivities my lady!

And no I don't! I agree we will share it out together.
Just like we share everything else. Heh!
Come to think of it, I wouldn't mind being a kept man at all!

So, *I'll stay home if you like"*

<u>MELANIE</u>

"It's an idea!
You are silly sometimes Simon... but I do love you".

<u>SIMON</u>

" And I love you too...very much"

<u>DIRECTION</u>

At this point they have a short loving kiss:

<u>SIMON</u> (Continues:)

"Which as it happens works out very well...
Especially if we decide to make some lovely brown babies!

But you are right: it is something we would have to work out very
carefully...
So that we can both play our part in caring for her, him or them!"

<u>DIRECTIONS</u>

With that Mel hits Simon gently with a rolled up magazine and they
hug.

Then the mood changes for a while.
Then both get a little more serious..

Mel opens up a cupboard and she begins to search out the right shoes for
her outfit.

<u>MELANIE</u> (Continues)

"But I do worry sometimes, about how they might be treated here in
England. Don't you ever worry about that Simon?
Just a little?"

DIRECTION

Simon sits back down on the bed for a while:
He speaks thoughtfully.

SIMON

"Things have changed Mel, and are continually changing for the good!

And what's more we'll be great parents!
We'll fight all the way to make things good for them and for us..

Don't worry Mel... it will be alright..
We'll make sure of it.

No – one will hurt them.. ever. We'll see to that"

DIRECTION

Simon continues, but this time more Light-heartedly.

SIMON

"As to how many, we will decide that when the time comes..

We may have twins, or triplets!
So we may not have a choice in the matter!
Can you imagine?

We never can know what's in store for us!"

MELANIE

"Gosh I never thought of that possibility.
You are scaring me now!
Do you have twins in your family?

SIMON

" Not that I know of...But who can tell, there could be way back..
Or some distant cousin might maybe?

226

Anyhow: whatever is to be, the gods of the future will decide for us"

DIRECTIONS

Simon stands again .The pair hug lovingly, and cheerfully.
By now Mel has found her shoes, which she holds in her hands:

Mel becomes serious again. She sits on the edge of the bed to put her shoes on.

The following is said very thoughtfully, considered and seriously..

MELANIE

"You are right Simon.
We will...

We will fight all the way.
No – one will ever hurt them. There's been enough hurt."

DIRECTION
There is a pause, followed by a serious voiced Mel saying:

"I love you Simon."

SIMON

"And I love you too Melanie who likes to be called Mel"

Simon puts his arms around Melanie again.
They kiss.
They both face the audience.

Melanie sings.
'WE'LL FIGHT ' (FULL VERSION VOCAL)

Eventually Simon joins in. The song ends with Simon and Melanie holding one another. Tight.

Scene Sixteen Ends

SCENE SEVENTEEN Begins

SETTING

Opens onto an Empty Stark darkened stage.

DIRECTIONS

A white older male figure dressed as a doctor in a white coat appears.
He is **standing up high** looking down upon Melanie and Simon..
Almost as if he standing on a graduated stairway
(One that grows narrower as it reaches its' pinnacle.)

He is holding a stethoscope and a clipboard.

Simon and Melanie are holding fast to one another.
As we left them.
They are looking upwards to him.

The doctor appears as an almost ethereal God like entity.
A somewhat dismembered figure with an echoing voice.

He addresses Simon and Melanie, as they hold on to one another
tightly.

GOD LIKE / DOCTOR FIGURE / PRESENCE

DIALOGUE

" I'm afraid it is bad news....   Echoing into silence>

The I. V. F. (pause) the problem is...   Fading into silence>

Nothing more we can do...   ibid.

We could try again...I suppose.   ibid.

However I wouldn't advise it.   ibid.

You have suffered so much trauma.   ibid.

There is little or no guarantee...   ibid.

Adoption..	*ibid.*
Fostering.	*Fading into silence*
There are always options.	*Echoing*
Let me reassure you.	*ibid.*
The emotional impact...	*ibid.*
We could offer counselling I suppose.	*ibid.*

You could make an appointment in the future if you so wish..
Just call my receptionist.

Yes counselling...

I suppose we could try again.	*Echoing >*

So that's it I suppose. I have to go, I am rather busy."

DIRECTIONS

Melanie and Simon have been listening intently.
At first they move slightly apart.

At each revelation they unravel a little bit further.
They are slowly letting go of one another, until eventually they are
completely separated.

When the 'Doctor' figure has finished speaking:

The music begins very softly.

Melanie begins to sing very softly and sadly.
As a requiem.

Reprise of **'WE'LL FIGHT'** *(A Softer slower version/ Partial Vocal/*
Partial Instrumental)

Simon joins in singing Very slowly and sadly..
Gradually they move away eventually standing far apart.

The singing stops and the **_instrumental version_** takes over, wafting across the stage between them.

As the music plays, it is as if it is moving them apart.

In tandem the two draw apart; until they stand alone looking towards one another, then slowly they turn face the opposite wings of the stage.

The music fades, as if to demonstrate how they have lost heart.

They walk away deliberately from one another, heads down in silence. They leave the stage.

The scene falls into silence and complete darkness.

<u>**Scene Seventeen Ends**</u>

SCENE EIGHTEEN Begins

SETTING

Halls of residence on Campus.
In a Bed - Sit Room; with single bed, desk, chair, wardrobe and small dressing table.

DIRECTIONS

Mel is now a Full Time Student. She is casually dressed in jeans, and blouse.

Melanie is sitting at the cheap desk surrounded by books and papers. She is writing, bent over an old word processor, which has a tiny screen. Mel is peering in order to see what she is writing.

The room is crammed with stuff: Her life's belongings.
Suitcases and boxes, clothes, papers and books fill the room.

There is a knock at the door…Melanie calls out:

MELANIE

"Yes, who is it?"

DIRECTION

A voice calls out from behind the door.

JENNI

"It's me. Jen of course!"

DIRECTION

Mel gets up from the desk to open the door.

Jenni is standing at the door. She is a young student; maybe white maybe not. Jenni is similarly dressed.
Jenni walks past Mel and into the room, she looks around, as if she is looking for something.

Mel goes back to what she was writing.
Jenni is bouncy, friendly and talkative.

DIALOGUE

JENNI

"How's it going then?"

DIRECTION

Jen now sits on the edge of the desk peering at the word processor and fiddling with some papers. Jen doesn't wait for an answer, and Mel doesn't give one.

JENNI continues:

"There's been loads of telephone calls for you, you know.
Seemingly from the same person each time!
Whoever it is, he's keen!

What going on then? Something I should know about eh?
You been incommunicado or what?
Didn't anyone tell you?

Anyhow tell me! Dish the dirt.
So, what's up? And how's it really going?"

DIRECTION

Again, Jenni doesn't wait for an answer to any of her questions:
And Mel doesn't give any.
Mel pushes Jen gently off the desk.
Jen takes no notice and still continues to wander about and asking questions that she doesn't wait for answers to.

Finally Jen wanders over to the bed…. She plonks herself on it, after collecting one of Melanie's apples on her way from a bowl on the side of the small dressing table. ..
Jen starts to munch on it…but not with much enthusiasm. Nevertheless she makes herself comfortable. Jenni continues:

JENNI

"You coming out then? Or what?

What's this then?
(Picking up an old apple core lying on the desk)

Still existing on bits of fruit alone I see!
You have to eat properly you know.. Like real food..
Pizza or something!"

DIRECTIONS

Jenni now starts rooting around the bedside table looking for
something else to eat...
Mel stops what she is doing and at last gives up writing in order to
answer Jenni.

MELANIE

"If you must know it's going terribly!
As to your advice:
No, I don't have to eat real food especially what you call real food.
I don't even like Pizza much!

And as to your other question:
No. No one mentioned any calls for me... Which is not surprising, as I
haven't left this room all afternoon; so I haven't seen any one who
might tell me!

DIRECTION (Mel takes a deep breath, and calms down)

Look Jen I'm really stretched here. And, lovely as it is to see you yet
AGAIN, you know, I have seen you everyday for the past I don't know
how many months, so, I would think you could do without my
company for a day or so while I get this work DONE!

I have to get on, and I have to get on now! If I'm going to pass this
Unit...I'm not even sure I'll get it in in time. Maybe I should just give
up!"

DIRECTION

Mel points somewhat over dramatically to the word processor.
Melanie now relents somewhat and follows suit to plonk herself on the bed next to Jenni.
Mel now seems somewhat dejected, as she slouches in the corner.

JENNI

"Mel you are just being over dramatic!
How could you lock yourself away from your best mate!
Essay or no essay!

We all have work to do you know!
You just take it all too seriously...
Anyhow; You of all of us have nothing to worry about..
You too good to fail.. And you should know it by now."

DIRECTION

Jen gives Mel a quick hug. Jen continues:

JENNI

"Come on Mel don't worry so, let's go out for a short time, get a bite to eat.. And have a change of scene.
It will do you good and me too. I'm starving...Why else would I be eating bits of your apple eh?

I'm telling you.
You take it all too seriously you know...
Too damn to heart and all....

As for passing this particular unit or any other for that matter actually you're streets ahead of any of us.. You'll pass mark my words... No problemo

Me I just do enough to scrape through...enough is enough, don't you know?" (Last words are uttered in feigned 'posh' English accent)

DIRECTION

Melanie brightens up a little at this show of confidence...she sits up.

234

MELANIE

" You really think so Jen? Thanks Jen. You're a good friend you know"

JENNI

"All part of the service. Now stop being soppy. You know I wouldn't say so if I didn't think so...don't you?"

MELANIE (Said now sitting upright)

"O.K, I suppose you are right.
About going out...not so sure about the rest of it though.

Sorry about the outburst.
I just have to make good here.. I have nothing else..

I'll have to take care of myself for the rest of time.
Start from scratch again; so I have to make rale good"

DIRECTION

Mel tails off . She is quiet.
She then brightens up again.

JENNI

" We all have to do that Mel! You not the only one you know.
Not many silver spoon merchants roaming around this Uni I can vouch. We not at some dreaming spire joint are we? Eh?
That's one of the main reasons we all here though, innit?
To get off the bottom of the dung heap Ain't that the truth?
Any how, enough of that."

MELANIE

" I'm so sorry Jen ...I know you all do.

Look, thanks for caring Jen, and putting up with me.
I'm just feeling so stressed... it's silly really.

I know we are all in the same boat...

Look, I'll just save this stuff; switch off, and then we'll get going."

DIRECTION

Melanie leaves the bed to walk across to the desk.
She sits down at the desk..

Jenni gets up too and follows, going across to the word processor.
Jenni stares at it intently.
Meanwhile Mel saves her work and turns off the word processor

MELANIE

" O.K that's done.
So, let's go out for that bite to eat. You never know, maybe we can find
something other than Pizza eh?

You're right it won't hurt to leave off for a while.
It is probably a good thing.
I shall come back to it all with fresh eyes eh?"

DIALOGUE

JENNI

" God Mel how do you manage with that thing?
You must have good eyes to see anything on that tiny screen!
It's out of the Ark… So what's wrong with Pizza eh?"

MELANIE

" I just not keen, I think it's the cheese or something, it sometimes
makes me feel bilious. So I eat fruit and stuff… it's safer."

JENNI

"Oh! Weird…anyway, I'm surprised you can see anything at all on
this thing…Never mind write essays! What you need is a proper
computer.
Like we can use in the library..

In fact most people have their own now..
Even me!"

MELANIE

"I know, but I think this is all I can afford.
Still, it does do the job... Just about I have to admit."

JENNI

" Can't your parents give you a hand?
They not short of a bob or two eh"

MELANIE

" Not many mature students seem to get help from their parents, not
that I know of.
And mine wouldn't help me out whatever age I was.

But especially not now, as I am now also officially a failed wife.
A disgrace even! There's no chance.
I've made my bed it seems, and now I have to lie on it!"

JENNI

" God Mel, Sounds like they are out of the ark too.

Anyhow, back to practicalities.

Where on earth <u>did</u> you get this word processor from?
I thought they have been defunct for years!
I'm surprised you found one still working.

You need to get with it girl.

And as for the failed wifey bit!
Give me strength, what are they religious nuts or what?"

DIRECTIONS

Again Jenni has no interest in any answers.
She now jumps back onto the bed.

237

Mel stays at the desk.

Excitedly Jenni continues to speak: Now, waving her arms about, like a conductor, all that's missing is the baton.

JENNI

"Look Mel, I know a guy who's upgrading his computer, so he's selling his old kit for a good deal.

He's a real geek, loves his technology; so he's always right up to date. Which means his old computer isn't that old, a good buy I can tell you!

I can introduce you to him if you like.

You never know; play your cards right and you could get a very good deal if you know what I mean?

He's kind of cute in a nerdy sort of way..
Anyhow that's your type isn't it?"

DIRECTIONS

Jenni laughs, but Mel turns around to look at Jen with a grimace;
Mel than speaks to Jen in a serious tone:

MELANIE

" I don't think so Jen.
I am not interested, and I don't have a type. Whatever that means.
So you can forget that angle.

I'm just going to stick to my work, get a good job and have a good life..
No complications from now on.

And that means no guys. Especially"

JENNI (Said whilst pulling herself bolt upright.)

"Ok Mel calm down. I know.. only joking.
Heh though! You still need a computer innit?

238

I could ring him, tell him you're interested.
It would make your life so much easier. You have to admit.
Do your essays quicker, so you could go out more!
Trust me..
And then maybe you wouldn't be so tetchy eh?"

DIRECTION

Mel starts to think, and soften to the idea.
She begins to look interested.

JENNI (Continues:)

In my first year I used to rely on the library computers too.
All that queuing 'round the block is no fun.
What with everyone looking to finish to the same deadline.
I tell you it's no good for the nerves Mel...

As for that word processor it is ridiculous! you'll end up with bottle glasses girl..
Not a good look I would say!"

DIRECTIONS

Things lighten up again.. and they both giggle.

MELANIE

" Well when you put it that way! I can see your point. Literally.

All right Jen you've convinced me.
But I still not sure I could afford it."

JENNI

" Don't worry, I've told you he'll do you a good deal..
And with No strings Mel!

Straight up.
He's a good guy really.
You could probably pay him up in instalments.

It's all up front and kosha like.

Shall I give him a call for you?
God, I wish I could afford one of those mobile 'phones... like those city
guys have.

Can you imagine not having to queue up in some public corridor?
Plus, not having everyone poking their noses into your private stuff
innit?
One day eh Mel?

When we have that high flying job and city pad..!
Won't be long.. But first we have to get you this deal..
I'll sort it out"

DIRECTIONS

With that Jenni bounces up from the bed, and heads for the door.
Jen leaves the room.
She can be heard off stage...talking loudly on the wall 'phone.
Mel takes the chance to continue to reorganise her papers and her desk.

JENNI

" Heh Josh .. How's it going eh?"

(Space)

"I got a buyer for your computer! Straight up.
Her name's Mel."

(Pause)

"She's here in halls, she's just along the corridor from me"

(Space)

"OK I'll tell her." (Space) *"Yes. Great."* (Space)

"Never, you did?" (Space)

"Sooo you know her!"   (Space)

"Ok see you soon"

DIRECTION

Meanwhile, whilst Jen is talking; Mel stands up and goes across to the bed. Mel gets on her knees.

She begins to scramble under her bed to look for her shoes. In the search, other stuff is soon strewn all over the floor, which has been taken from under the bed.

DIALOGUE

MELANIE   (To herself)

"Now where are those shoes?
I can never find anything in this stupid room."

DIRECTIONS

Meanwhile Jenni has put the 'phone down and rushed excitedly back into Mel's room calling out...

JENNI

" Heh Mel, you dark horse!

Josh said he knows you, that you all went out together a couple of times last term?"

MELANIE

" Oh Josh? He's the guy!

Well I don't know him that well..
No, not really.

I remember him but only in a crowd, maybe we went for a meal or something.. I can't remember.

Nothing much to it really."

JENNI

" Well he remembers you! Really well.
You certainly made an impression on him!

 Oh, whatever.

Anyhow; he's only 'round the corner, he's popping over just for a chat,
just to see whether you would be interested.

He seems very keen, I think a good deal is on the table if you know
what I mean eh?"

DIRECTIONS

Mel shoots a pointed look towards Jenni..

DIALOGUE

MELANIE

" Now Jen, Don't start all that again!"

JENNI

" No I'm not Mel. Honest!"
I know! I get the picture innit.
Strictly business Mel…

The computer! Mel, That's all I meant..
To sell off the computer at a good price."

MELANIE

" I should hope so. Right, so we're not going out for a meal after all?

Only I can't find my shoes in this lot anyway so maybe that's a good
ting!"

JENNI

" Yeah, But maybe we will later on, after Josh has been eh? Cos I'm proper starving"

MELANIE

" You're always proper starving!
Still, I have to go out sometime...innit, as you would say
So I suppose I'd best find them anyhow.

I think   (Mel pulls out some stuff... then one shoe)
And here's the other."   (Mel pulls out the other shoe)

DIRECTION

Mel sits on the edge of the bed to put on her shoes.

MELANIE

"I'll pop them on just in case we ever decide what we are doing!"

DIRECTION

At this point there is a knock at the door.
It is Josh. (Dressed in sneakers, a T Shirt and jeans, under his coat)

He doesn't wait to be asked to come in, he just does; as the door is still ajar from Jenni's to and froing.

So, Josh comes straight in, closing the door behind him with his foot. Josh is carrying a very large Pizza, and has cans of soft drinks sticking out from the pockets of his coat.

DIALOGUE

JOSH

"Aye! You were expecting me ladies?
Anyone for Pizza?   (Josh waves the Pizza around flamboyantly.)
Here's one I made earlier"

DIRECTION

Josh laughs in a pleasant easy way at his own weak joke.

DIALOGUE
JENNI

" Hi Josh, you were quick, and a Pizza too. It's as if it were planned!"

JOSH

" Any thing for the ladies, you know me Jen!

(Josh turns his attention directly to Mel.
His eyes light up somewhat. Josh clearly likes Mel.)

Hi Mel, long time no see eh?
You kind of disappeared off the radar after last term!"

DIRECTION

Mel looks down with a mixture of embarrassment, shyness and impatience.

She does not seem content with the way things are developing.
Panicking somewhat Mel starts to usher Jenni and Josh towards the door..

DIALOGUE

MELANIE

"OK that's it. Look, I've changed my mind; maybe this isn't such a good idea after all.

A few minutes ago I was happily working away, now we seem to have a party going on.

I think maybe you and Josh should go back to yours, enjoy the Pizza, and I will catch up with you another time!
I don't even like Pizza!"

JOSH

" Oh come on Mel! Don't be like that..

Look it's hot <u>now</u>. No one wants to eat a cold Pizza, now do they?
Well not unless you are hung over of a morning with nothing else in
the fridge that is, then that's a very different matter.."

DIRECTIONS

Jenni and Josh both laugh and begin to look pleadingly at Melanie.
In unison they plead..

DIALOGUE

JENNI & JOSH (Said in unison)

"Please, pretty please."

JOSH

" And, apart from that, I can definitely give you a good deal on that
computer... you don't have to pay it all up front you know.

 We can make arrangements and stuff...if you know what I mean."

DIRECTIONS

MELANIE

Gives Josh a look to kill.

JOSH

" Oops! O.K I get the message!

What I mean is: Instalments....As .. Just Friends. Eh?

SO! Mates rates, no strings!

Now! That's the business part done

Can we eat this Pizza?.. My hands are burning from it and my belly's
rumbling empty!"

<u>MELANIE</u> (Relenting)

" OK As long as you understand the terms! That there'll be no funny business. OK?"

<u>DIRECTION</u>

Josh nods energetically whilst placing his hand on his heart.

<u>JOSH</u>

"Hand on heart Mel, honest. Now, can we eat this damn Pizza?"

<u>MELANIE</u> (Softening & smiling)

"OK seeing as to how that's understood and is crystal clear, I guess we may as well.

I'll get some plates out for you, as for the computer; I'll try to pay in one go.
That's if I like it and it's one I want, <u>and</u> I can somehow afford the price..."

<u>DIRECTION</u>

Mel walks across to a cupboard and gets out some paper plates, and paper napkins..
She moves over some papers from the side of her desk, and puts the plates onto the table.
Mel then takes the Pizza from Josh.
Mel puts that down too. She opens it.
Mel then finds a knife from a drawer.

She begins to slice it up, and pops a piece onto each plate.
Mel hands out the paper plates to Jen & Josh leaving one for herself.
She continues:

<u>MELANIE</u>

"<u>And</u> I want to see a proper receipt, where it came from and all kinds of things like that. All kosher, as Jen would say!

246

Look Josh you can sit on this chair,
And Jenni you can go back onto the bed...
(Jen sits down on the bed, with her plate at the side of her.)

There we go. That's the best I can do.

We'll have to use fingers though!
But we do have some napkins to help us clean up a tad"

DIRECTIONS

They all laugh. Mel then pulls a cushion from the bed and perches on the cushion on the floor with her paper plate balanced on her knee.

MELANIE

"What you all laughing at?"

JOSH

"Nothing Mel, only you would think eating Pizza needs cutlery!

No Probs. Lady Mel!
Paper plates at the ready. How's that for being prepared?

That's what I love..
I mean like about you Mel..
Very proper, resourceful and forceful woman eh Jen?
And look!"

DIRECTION

Josh gets up from the chair; he puts his plate on the chair for a moment in order to pull some cans out from his coat pockets.

JOSH (Continues)

"Like magic rabbits!
Sorted or what Lady Mel?
And no cups required either!"

MELANIE (Laughing)

" As you say Josh.. Sorted"

JENNI

"Josh, just shut up! If you keep winding her up like that she will chuck us out and then we on cold pizza for sure!

Sorry Mel, he'll behave himself from now on I promise."

MELANIE

"No Jen, it's me who's sorry...
I know I can come across as a bit stuffy and all...
I am trying to lose it. Loosen up, as you would say.

OK, look for true, I think I would like this computer.
It's good of you Josh to offer it to me..

I just; well everything is getting to me at the moment...
I really need good grades..
And you're right Jen; it would help me get them. and to work quicker."

JOSH (Said whilst picking up his Pizza in order to sit back down on his chair)

" No worries Mel, you doing me a favour too! I need the dosh...just a tad (Josh Laughs)
But, It's true, you do need to seriously loosen up, maybe we could..."

DIRECTIONS

Josh is cut short, there is a knock at Mel's door again..

DIALOGUE

JENNI

"Heh this is turning into a party after all!"

JOSH

" Yeah, a Mel special, teetotal and very refined.
Maybe I should be butler!"

DIRECTION

Josh gets up from the chair and says this whilst prancing around in a
pseudo 'genteel' manner. He puts his Pizza down again.
Slightly teasing Mel, Josh bows and takes it upon himself to open her
door.
Mel laughs at him, and then looks aghast as she sees Simon standing
at the doorway

Mel eventually gathers her wits enough to speak.

DIALOGUE

MELANIE

" What are you doing here? How the heck did you find me?"

SIMON (Said in a serious, almost apprehensive manner)

" Hello Mel. How are you?

(Said in a quiet voice. Simon doesn't wait for an answer)

It wasn't hard...you left an easy paper trail..
Plus your Mother..."

MELANIE (Interrupting him)

"That woman never could mind her own business...she shouldn't have
told you anything.

You can't just waltz back into my life.. Disrupting everyting.
Not even for a second..."

DIRECTIONS

Mel's voice begins to rise, as she becomes more upset, and panicky.
She is looking up at Simon in disbelief.

Mel is on the verge of tears.

Simon moves forward tentatively, making himself to be half in the room and half out in the hallway.

Simon looks uncomfortable at his reception: and Josh & Jennie are also looking a bit taken aback. Everyone now appears to be slightly embarrassed.

DIALOGUE

SIMON

"Look Mel, I haven't come to upset you.

Firstly, I wanted to see if you were all right.

Secondly, we do need to talk...

We have things to sort out, practical things... and, well you know"

DIRECTIONS

All the old wounds begin to resurface and emotions become high.. Melanie appears very upset and shocked. She is now shaking.

Melanie scrambles up from her cushion on the floor in order to be face to face with Simon. She almost throws the paper plate and pizza onto her desk.

DIALOGUE

MELANIE

" All I know is choices were made, and that's that.

You come here all smiles on your face, and expect me to sit down wit you, talking, as if nothing happened...

Just Go!

Who do you think you are?"

<u>SIMON</u> (Now it is Simons' turn to be taken aback. He takes a deep breath. Maybe he had not been expecting such a reception from Mel?)

" Well; for one thing I think I am someone who actually cares about you...and what happens to you. That's who I am."

<u>DIRECTIONS</u>

At This point Jenni gasps out loud, as she realises whom Simon might be.
Everyone now looks to one another with perplexed expressions.
It dawns on them all, that the party (that never really was) is now certainly over.

Jenni is the first to regain her composure and respond to the situation:

Jenni gets up from the bed and grabs Josh by the arm....pulling him towards the doorway.

<u>DIALOGUE</u>

<u>JENNI</u>

"Look Mel we really should be going.

Just remembered we should be somewhere else by now.
Things to do; people to annoy and all. You know how it is.
The student life eh? It's all go, go, go.
So we should now get gone, gone, gone eh Josh?

We'll leave you all to it...
Come on Josh, we can eat this in the bar..."

<u>JOSH</u>

" Well me personally I don't have anything much to do right now"

<u>JENNI</u>

" Oh yes you do!
Remember we said we'd meet up with the others eh?"

JOSH

" Others? Other who? What?"

JENNI (Directed to Simon)

" The boy a bit hung over...not too sharp at the moment.
You know what some students can be like,

Not me though..
I'm like Mel here. Strictly Teetotal!"

JOSH

"Well that's news to..."

JENNI (Cuts in fast)

" To be shared, and celebrated... I know I know. Great isn't it?
I feel so cleansed and sharp nowadays!
You should try it Josh! It'll make a new man of you yet.

I try to spread the good news daily you know!   (Aimed at Simon)
A regular missionary that's me. Eh Josh?"

DIRECTIONS

Jenni pulls Josh harder by his arm and tugs him towards the door.
They both squeeze past Simon.
Josh is still looking a bit 'put out'

Now Josh is more concerned about his Pizza than anything else.
Josh makes sure he grabs as much of the Pizza as he is able, together
with some fresh paper plates, and a couple of napkins for good measure.

JENNI

"Come on.. (Said Forcibly to Josh)
We'll see you later Mel eh?

Nice to meet you... er I didn't get your name"

SIMON

"Sorry, I didn't give it. I'm .."

MELANIE (Interrupts)

"You don't need to know Jen,
You won't be meeting again.
I'll catch you both later, in the bar O.K?"

JOSH

"Hang on Jen.. What about my cans?"

JENNI

"Forget them!... I'll get you a soft drink in the bar.
Just take the hint!"

DIRECTIONS

With that Jenni & Josh leave, in a bit of a jumble.
There is a silent hiatus until Melanie and Simon are sure Jenni & Josh
have truly gone out of earshot, and that they are alone.

SIMON

"They seemed nice. Very err, lively.
Look Mel, there was no need for that. Are you ashamed of us?
What are you trying to hide from?

So, I gather you're not too pleased to see me?"

DIRECTIONS

There is now another long drawn out silence.
They stand in the tiny room facing one another as they once did.
This time the scene changes/blends in to the bar scene as if in a
dream....

Scene Eighteen Ends / Blends into Scene Nineteen.

<u>SCENE NINETEEN Begins/ Blended from Eighteen</u>

<u>SETTING STUDENT BAR / DREAM LIKE SEQUENCE</u>

<u>DIRECTIONS</u>

Josh, Jenni and others are milling about at and around the Students' bar.
They are in the background. Some dancing to <u>silence.</u>
Quietly like ghosts...As in a dream like setting.

Mel and Simon are centre stage: The spotlight is on them alone:
Simon takes Mel's hand.. She gently but determinedly pulls it away.

<u>DIALOGUE</u>

<u>SIMON</u>

" I loved you so much Mel, you were my one and only true love."

<u>MELANIE</u>

" I don't know what you're trying to say to me,
This time it's the end of the chase..
So Just go.."

<u>DIRECTIONS</u>

SIMON turns without a word, and walks away to the sidelines.
He turns again holding his arms outstretched towards Mel.

Mel 'mutates' into the dream- like bar scene.
She faces away from Simon to the audience

Mel sings the song <u>'JUST GO' (FULL VOCAL VERSION).</u>

Throughout the song Simon continues to back off the stage.
He becomes less lit /fading slowly from the scene.
Simons' hands eventually fall to his side.
Before the end of the song he has gone completely.
Jenni & Josh and others in the dream like state in the Students' bar
begin to dance out the lyrics... <u>SET DANCE ROUTINE></u>

254

DIRECTIONS

The scene/ setting comes/mutates back into reality/ into the now.
Not dream like anymore.

The latter part of the song finishes in real time / the now.

Then people mill around going up to the bar and there is now a melee of
chat and noises in the background

Jenni and Josh walk over to Mel.

DIALOGUE

JENNI

"Your visitor gone then Mel? He seemed nice...but a tad, well staid.
Not that there's anything wrong with that. Staid can be good.
Respectable and all that. You get me?"

JOSH

" Yeah, Mel I wanna know who the competition is"

MELANIE (Mel's voice is somewhat hard, business like even, in her
attempt to move on)

" He's just someone I used to know... It didn't work out, that's all.
He's no competition. Because there is no competition.

Like I told Jen,
It's just me and my work from now on Josh.
Just me, myself And I!

So, now.
Let's sort out this computer business. When can I see it?"

JOSH

" Well right now is good for me. You coming too Jen?"

JENNI

" Yep for sure…"

DIRECTIONS

Josh turns and walks to the door. The women however don't follow, and as Josh reaches the doorway Jenni calls out to him.

DIALOGUE

JENNI

" Heh Josh, on second thoughts, we'll catch up with you in a while. Just got some girl talk to do OK."

JOSH

" Whatever ladies!

I'll get the kit booted up ..
I'll see you later…
You know where I am. Don't be too long eh?"

DIRECTION

Jenni excitedly pulls Melanie over to a table…They sit down.

DIALOGUE

JENNI

" You ok Now Mel? So what's the story?

After that, he's gone for good, for sure now.
I didn't tell Josh who he was.

I mean I don't know for sure myself but I kinda guessed.
I think even Josh may have worked it out and had an idea too.
But then again, maybe not! You know what he's like eh?
Not the most observant sleuth in life's game of cluedo, more like no clue derh…. To be fair"

MELANIE (Spoken softly and dreamily)

" Yes, I guess you're right on both counts.

For true! He has gone for sure now. For ever 'til...death"

DIRECTION

Mel sighs...Her voice trails off. She doesn't finish the word or indeed the sentence.

MELANIE

"It had to be done, and you know what Jen?

No – one should rely on relationships to work out for them to achieve happiness...
You have to make your own happiness.

There's no one you can rely on for that.

So now, I just want to concentrate on my work and get good results.
I need to make my own way without distractions.

I have to make something of myself... whoever myself is.
No more pipe dreams. No more trusting.
No more trying for happiness, happy families and such like
It just don't exist...
Not in my world anyhow.

(Mel breaks off. She Pauses. Mel places her hand on top of Jen's hand.)

It's all too late for that Jenni. All too late"

DIRECTIONS

Melanie stares into space..
Time stops again.

Moira's voice comes across from the ether.

MOIRA

"You listen to me Melanie. You go back now. You go back to him!

257

You'll never achieve anyting like dis.
You thrown away your passport to everything..

Look at you ...Hair all frizzed up. And have you bin in de sun?

You just annoder blacker than black girl now, just hanging around.
Just annoder girl waiting to be preyed on.

All that so called education you so fond of getting mean nothing out
there in the world you know! Not for a girl such as you.
I can tell you! You won't get no white job out there, and such.

No job can replace being married to a respectable man like Simon!

He have a good job and all kinds of ting like that you know.
A profession even, just like Daddy!
You gone and ruined everything now.
And after all we done for you.
Wedding and all such ting like that.

What more could you have wanted Melanie?
That's what I want to know eh?

You not respectable no more Melanie... No more.
Standing on your own two feet. I hear nutten of the like.
More like falling down and out.
And you will my girl.
You will fall good and hard.
Idiocy! What you tink yuh doin?

You gone and broke your Mothers' heart that what you dun...
And after all we did for you...Look on yuh.
You end up alone! In some teeny room and such, wit rough friends like
dat! Dem look like low life to meh.

Such a _fine_ Wedding and all. Everyone praised it yuh know!
You're Daddy wasting all that money on you and all.

All for nothing now Melanie...All those years I cared for you, bring
you up right to be a lady. An now look on yuh. It all for nutten"

JENNI (In the now/ present)

258

"Mel! Mel! Where you gone?
You daydreaming or what?

Look, You know what Mel; what you say...
You may be right.

But it wouldn't work for me.
I like to be part of a couple too much. (If you know what I mean).

But I do get your point.

Look at all that stuff we're learning about, how things used to be.

God, in those days once you married then, you had to stay married.
No matter what. And I mean no matter!

And that must have been hard... real hard.
Glad we not around then eh Mel?"

DIRECTION

The girls stare into space. Contemplating their fate.

JENNI Continues:

"Maybe you just need time to figure things out...
To heal up a little;
Then you'll feel differently"

MELANIE

"I guess so...Maybe.
I don't know anything at the moment.
Not for sure.

Anyhow, like Josh said, I maybe also just need to free up a bit.
I've had enough down times...
I need to make some good memories for the future.

So this is a perfect time to start.
Oh no! speak of the devil"

DIRECTIONS

At this point Josh comes striding back into the bar area.
He is waving a poster at the girls.

JOSH

" Hey Ladies, I know you can't possibly be done yet…
With the girl talk and all.
But the kit is now ready for your inspection, My Lady Mel"

DIRECTIONS

Josh makes a low exaggerated flourishing bow to Mel.
He then plonks himself in between the two women, spreading out the
poster onto the table.

JOSH Continues:

"And what's more I also wanted to show you this in time!

There's some sort of Gig here tonight, which I grant you is not
unusual, but what is unusual is; you all could take part!

And you ladies could make up, add to, your marks at the same time!

Genius or what? And so cool!

You know what I was saying to you earlier that you need to loosen up
Mel? Well how's about starting now, with this?

I mean what more could you want?
It even enhances your work and maybe ups' your grades that you so
fond of at the same time!!! "

DIRECTION
(Jenni and Mel look dubious)

JOSH

"You don't have to thank me all at once!
I tell you! It'll be great! What more could you ask for?"

JENNI

" Watch out! (Jen ducks)
Another Josh special idea coming, or do I mean disaster?"

DIRECTIONS

Josh holds up the Poster advertising a '*1920's night*' dance to be held in
the bar that night...

JOSH (continues)

"Ha ha, so witty. Not.
Oh you of little faith!
This idea is completely bullet proof I assure you!

Now this event would most definitely benefit from the attendance of
you two fine ladies.
And my good self of course..

I mean ladies like yourselves need a willing escort.
Am I right or am I right?
You can thank me later in _whatever_ manner you may see fit?
Pizza, beer, clothes washing, _anything_ that springs to your minds!"

DIRECTION

Josh stands up to deliver another flourishing bow.
This time it is directed at both women, and is even more exaggerated.

JOSH

"So in conclusion, as they say, as it is part of your course Lady Mel,
you would effectively be working AND having the prescribed by Dr.
Josh fun, all at the same time!"

DIRECTION

Josh dances around in a foolish light hearted way as he speaks.

JOSH (continues)

"How cool is that?
What do you think? What do you think?" (Said in his best 'cartoon' voice)

DIRECTIONS

Mel laughs out loud. Then so does Jenni.

MELANIE

" You are kidding me!
Josh, you are priceless, incorrigible!"

JOSH

" Well I don't know if that's a good thing, a bad thing or even English.
But it's probably true!

It really says here 'If you perform, it can go towards your marks'
So I'm not making it up!

So how's about it? You all coming?
We'll have a blast...
And you don't _have_ to perform; that is if you don't want to.
But that's rubbish as I think you should."

JENNI

" I agree with Josh. For once. Never happened before!
Heh Mel, You could do one of your songs. That really would be so cool."

DIRECTIONS

Melanie hesitates, but only for a while..
She looks at her two friends.
She nods her head then says:

MELANIE

"Why not ?
My new life... it has to start somewhere!
And here and now is as good as any other time. If not better.

I have to learn to ignore the doubts.
So why not start now?

Soooo....O.K if the girl from Mars says Yes
Then I say Yes"

JENNI

" Heh; Jenni says a BIG yes!
And it's not Mars, it's Venus. Now."

JOSH (Pulling the girls up to stand and trying to pick up both girls to swing them around in his arms):

"The ladies from Bog standard Uni say YES!

Now you are talking my language at last..."

DIRECTION

Josh runs out of steam and has to let the girls down unceremoniously..
To their amusement and pretended chagrin:

JOSH

"Phew. What you girls bin eating?
I'll have to ration that Pizza habit on you Jen.
So, tell me, a mere male, what the devil is it all about?"

DIRECTIONS

Jenni begins to read from the poster.

JENNI

"It says:
'Shows evidence of understanding the progress of women's suffrage...'

My God Mel? Why didn't we know about this before?"

DIRECTION

Josh buts in and then leans over to read the rest of the Poster.

JOSH

"Don't thank me ladies..
I reiterate I am just a genius..

Anyhow, you two will understand what it's going on about...
So that's what matters.
Sounds heavy stuff to me, the token male.

It also says:
'The most creative and entertaining offerings could be incorporated
into 'The Arts Independent Study Units' final mark...'

Whatever that is..
So you two _definitely_ doing that Unit?"

JENNI

" Of Course!"

JOSH

"Great! So we're set and good to go, and what's more if you do perform
we all get in for free, with the first drink free at the bar too!
Not that that has influenced my enthusiasm.
I've only just noticed that on the poster. Just now. For true.

In fact you may not know this. But I'm well known for my feminist
leanings.
Yes, I've always leant towards the ladies."

JENNI

"Josh. Stop talking rubbish! The more you rabbit on the worse it gets.

So that's decided. (Said to Mel)

Come on Mel. Let's do it... that song you've come up with...you could
use that, it's just right. Plus I've got a poem I could use up.

We've got a couple of hours to grab some costumes, and stuff.
Try to make it authentic. What do you think?

(Jenni looks thoughtful…)

I think I know where we can borrow some 20's stuff!
It's a bit short notice, but I can twist a few arms, and call in a few
favours, so we should be able to cobble together some sort of a decent
turn out."

DIRECTIONS

By now Jenni is jumping up and down with excitement.
She is grabbing Mel's hands.

"Come on Mel happy days, happy days!
Memories Mel! Memories."

MELANIE (Brightening up, touched by Jenni's spark)

"As you're in. I'm in."

Jenni turns to Josh

JENNI (In her bossy manner)

"Right. Josh.
We're off to search out some costumes:
So, we'll catch up with you later…"

DIRECTION

The girls start to leave; Jenni then turns back to Josh and says (almost
as an after thought and throwaway line) to him, over her shoulder:

JENNI

"By the way get yourself a tux or something.
You'll have to look the part. We not having you show us up!"

JOSH

"Are you two mad!
Where the hell will I get a tux at this late stage?
I'm just a poor Student at Bog Uni, not some toff at Oxbridge.

All I have to my name is two pairs of jeans and six T-shirts..
And a couple of pairs of pants!

I need to borrow some togs too!
Let me come along with you, I need help!"

JENNI

" You certainly do!
Did you say a couple? That's gross Josh!
I expect you only have two pairs of socks too!"

JOSH

" What ? What?
I'll think you'll find my wardrobe is perfectly sufficient for my needs!
I've never had any complaints…Well not up to now that is…"

DIRECTIONS

Mel and Jenni groan; whilst holding their noses in mockery and
laughter.

With that Mel & Jenni run to the door leaving Josh shaking his head…
and holding the Poster.
He's not sure if being left alone was quite what he had in mind.

Then Josh decides he has to follow. He runs after them, to off stage.

JOSH (Said to himself as he goes)

" By the way you two will have to find me a tux!
 I've no clue where to find one!
Just remember you don't want me to show you all up.

And what's more, what happened to that drink I was promised!"

The Scene Nineteen ends

266

SETTING: Opens in the Same Student Bar .
 Later that same Night.

At the far end of the room, there is a small stage, with sound
equipment on it.
The whole place has been 'tweaked' to give it a 1920's theme.

Most people have come along dressed in appropriate '20's Garb.

DIRECTIONS

There is a general hubbub of noise and some beat emanating from the
stage. (Use Just Go!)

Two tech guys are up on stage twiddling with the sound system, which
adds to the noise level.

The only difference to a normal night is that most of the girls and
guys are dressed in their versions of Nineteen -Twenties clothes.
Even Josh has managed to cobble together some sort of Dinner Suit
(Of a fashion!)

The scene is crowded. It is the usual melee.

There is a modest ' tweedy' nerdy, chap wearing glasses sitting at a
table to the side of the stage.
He has a bewildered look on his face as he juggles with papers.
He is the nights MC. (And partly an adjudicator?)

He is dealing with the list of the evenings running order.
It is beginning to defeat him, as some papers fall to the floor...

Centre stage Josh & Jenni are prominent, as is Melanie.
Melanie is carrying a bag on her shoulder.

A couple of Lecturers are standing as far from the stage as they can
get, with their backs to the wall trying to go unnoticed.
They have their briefcases on the floor besides them, which together with
their maturity somewhat gives them away.

They are holding drinks, and talking intently to one another.
They are trying not to look too serious, but failing.
Melanie walks across to the Female Lecturer, and begins a conversation with her.

Meanwhile, Jenni & Josh stroll off, over to the bar.

DIALOGUE

MELANIE

"Excuse me Ms Jones, sorry to bother you.
But, well I have.. I have a piece sort of prepared.
Is it possible for me to enter a submission at this late stage?

I mean it's just, well it's not. It's just a song.

But, it does have a serious intent to it!
Some content that is relevant to.. the criteria.

Some people like it. I mean.. The few who have heard it that is.
Well they seem to think it's ok"

FEMALE LECTURER. Ms. JONES

" Hello Mel. How are you?
It's good to see you here!   (Ms. Jones sounds a little surprised)

Yes, of course you can submit.
That shouldn't be a problem.

Just put your name down with Mr Brookes over there at the table by the stage..
Oh, and the title of your piece.. Together with a short description.

You can give a short resume of intent and content later on if you decide to submit the performance for accreditation."

MELANIE

"Really?"   (Sounding surprised at the ease of entering and maybe
                wishing it wasn't so)

MS JONES

" Yes Really..   (Said with a small laugh)
It's all quite informal.

A song you say.
It sounds fun.
Don't be so nervous. (She places her hand lightly on Mel's Lower arm)

As I said, just give your details to Mr Brookes over there at the table.

Mel, I assure you it will only count towards your marks if we all feel it
would benefit you.
Otherwise it's just for the fun of it. Ok?

That especially includes you too! If you're satisfied with how it goes,
then it counts. If not. It doesn't. Simple as that.

So, just go ahead and enjoy yourself! Hang on!
I may as well take a few details myself, whilst we're both here"

DIRECTION

Ms Jones takes a piece of paper out of her briefcase, which is lying on
the floor beside her.

Mel looks apprehensively across to Mr. Brookes, as she hands a piece of
paper with her details to Ms Jones.

MELANIE

" It's called _'Let's Step Back In Time'_"
As I said, it's just a song..."

MS JONES (Continues talking as she scribbles down the few details)

"Intriguing title!
Don't worry Mel, I promise...
It will only count towards your final mark if it really is to your
advantage...

As I said it is meant to be fun too, so enjoy!"

269

DIRECTION

Mel continues to look a little crest fallen, as Ms Jones hastily copies a few more details from Mel's paper.
Ms Jones hands the paper back to Mel.

MALE LECTURER. Mr DOWNES

" Mel, I don't know what you are worried about, your marks are way up there anyhow.. So it doesn't really matter, too much.

 AND I am sure it will be great!
Just go up there and have fun!"

MELANIE

" That's what everyone keeps saying to me; have fun.

 But what if I don't know how?
I really want to. I really do.

Anyhow, thanks for your encouragement.
I'll go over and give Mr Brookes my details."

DIRECTIONS

Mel turns to go over to Mr Brookes and the stage.
She begins to make her way over there.

Half- way Mel stops and the scene freezes.

Mummy/Moira's voice comes from the ether:

MOIRA

" What you doing now Melanie?
Making a show of yourself in public! Again!
You just another stupid black girl up there singing...
When you could have been a lady"

Grandma's voice cuts in to demand attention.

GRANDMA IN SPIRIT

"Don't listen to her Mel.
This is your chance to break away! Mel. Hear me out.

Remember, how we would sing when you was a baby?
Go sing like we used to Mel.. Sing your heart out.

Sing yourself forward away from all the heartache Mel.
I watching you girl Listening too!
Take no notice of her Mel!

You almost free girl.. You almost free of them all!"

MELANIE /TO The AUDIENCE/ SUSPENSION

"It looks kind of daunting up there to me, now I'm here.
I've never really sung in public before.
Not proper in public..

I mean to people who are not just friends or family.
Maybe I should give it a miss...

But if I do,
I know; I will never take the chance again"

DIRECTION

Mel begins to turn away as if she is changing her mind.

At this point Jenni and Josh call over to Mel...gesticulating.
They have guessed that Mel is having second thoughts..
They charge over to Mel.

Back in THE NOW

DIALOGUE

JENNI

" Don't you dare Melanie James!

271

We haven't gone to all this trouble, these clothes and everything, just for you to go cold on us!"

JOSH

" Yeah. Just look at the state of me! I look a right Pratt.

And you've no idea what I had to promise to get my hands on this tux!"   (Said whilst pulling at the jacket)

JENNI

" So that's what it is! I was wondering!"

JOSH

" Almost funny Jen! (He now turns his attention back to Mel)

Come on Mel, get a move on. You're up NEXT!
If you don't, we may have to pay up, for services rendered, if you know what I mean, tickets, and drinks.
Not that that matters too much. I mean I'm easy on that."

DIRECTION

(Said to cover up his slight embarrassment; especially as Jen gives him a dig with her elbow)

JOSH (Continues:)

"But, it would be a pity to lose out. Don't you all think?

Plus, we've already put your details down with Brookes' here; and given over the music from your bag for you earlier on.
Just a little light pilfering amongst friends...
Temporary of course!

Mr Brookes has you on next so that you've no time to change your mind! We thought of everything girl. All you got to do is sing!
You stuck with it now, there's no going back!"

DIRECTIONS

Mel gives Josh & Jenni a disapproving look!

JENNI

"Yeah, I know...
But needs must eh?

Oh, and here's your Photo I.D back.
Come on Mel give it a go!
Remember the I will if you will promise?

Well I kept my part of the bargain...
All done and dusted.

So now it's your turn to keep yours, in this music part of the night!

Plus, let's make those memories eh?"

DIRECTIONS

With that Jenni pushes the ID back into Mel's bag.
And both Josh and Jen gently push Mel towards the stage.

Mel's legs seem reluctant to move..
The tech guys have finished setting up and everything is ready.

LECTURER Ms JONES

(Said whilst witnessing the persuasions..)

"Come on Mel, you can do it..
Remember it is for fun too!"

DIRECTION

At this moment the Lecturer **Ms JONES** abandons her position as a wall- flower.
She walks across to Mel and she gently takes Mel's arm and guides Mel to the side of the stage..

Ms JONES (Whispers into Mel's ear)

*" Only if you want to **Mel**, but I think, like your friends here..*
That you <u>can</u> do it, and you should give it a go."

DIRECTION

Mel looks around taking in the scene.
Mr. Downes feels he may as well join in..
So he walks across to join the group.

Mr. DOWNES (Said in a bluff, but kind manner)

" Give it a go I always say.. Nothing much to lose eh?"

DIALOGUE

MELANIE

" Only the chance to look stupid in front of most of my year!

Come on Mel, It is now or never!   (Said to herself)

Oh what the hell!"   (Said out loud)

DIRECTIONS

With that Melanie clambers up onto the stage.
She throws her bag down to the floor by the side of the stage.

Josh and Jenni retreat to the centre of the main floor, as does Ms Jones
and Mr Downes:
Mr Brookes ticks her name from his list.
He then clambers up onto the stage and announces:

MR. BROOKES/ M.C. (Said rather shyly and in a bit of a bumbling manner)

"Erh right oh.
Right, so in this the musical part of this evenings erh … entertainment
Anyhow next up!
This is Melanie James.. (Said whilst looking across to Mel)

With a song she has composed herself..

Erh that is the Lyrics and Music...Sounds impressive.
So, She's in year three.

Erh, It's called   *(Said whilst sifting through his many lists)*
Em it's called, just bear with me. It's called"

DIRECTION

Mel looks across at Josh and Jenni who are giving her the thumbs up, as she moves next to Mr Brookes to stand at his side next to the microphone.

JOSH (Calls out)

" Oh for goodness sake, it's called '<u>Let's Step Back In Time</u>'!"

MR BROOKES

" Erh..... Yes I was just about to say that thank you!
The piece is called:
Yes. It <u>is</u> called:

'<u>Let's Step Back In Time</u>'. "

JOSH

" I told you Mel, they've got the music.
Just give them the nod!"

DIRECTION

Mel looks transfixed standing silently.
There is quite an uneasy pause.

At last Mel turns to the tech guys and nods, to indicate that she is ready for the backing track to begin>

Mr Brookes scrambles off stage: Just in time. It's all very awkward.

Voices call out and whoop encouragement>

DIALOGUE

JENNI

" Come on Mel.. Make those memories!"

JOSH

" Let the fun begin Mel. Yeah!"

DIRECTION

The music blasts out. >

'LET'S STEP BACK IN TIME' (FULL VOCAL VERSION)
SET DANCE SEQUENCE ensues on the dance floor.

Mel jumps down at one point from the stage to dance.

Most of the room joins in the dance.

Especially Jenni & Josh.

The two Lecturers Ms Jones & Mr. Downes eventually join in.
Latterly Mr. Brookes leaves his post and has a little shimmy.

When the music ends he sits back at his table in a slightly
embarrassed manner.

At the very end **everyone cheers** much to Melanie's surprise.
Mel looks astonished, but pleased.

The scene goes back to general melee/ noise/ beat.
(Use 'Let's Step Back In Time' Instrumental parts)

Josh and Jenni are back at the bar celebrating.
They raise their glasses to Mel.

Mel picks up her bag from the side of the stage.
She begins to walk towards Jenni & Josh.
Mel is happy.

The small Chap at the desk MC / Mr. Brookes waylays Mel before she
reaches Jenni & Josh.

DIALOGUE

Mr BROOKES

" Heh Mel, thanks for that. We were struggling for decent stuff up to now. It really helped the evening along.
 Pretty good I'd say...
You should get great marks!

It's Ms Jones watching you isn't it?
By her reaction and everyone else's I would say you are on to a winner!"

DIRECTION

Ms. Jones /Lecturer appears at their side at this moment. She overhears.

DIALOGUE

Ms JONES/ LECTURER

" It just so happens I agree with Mr. Brookes..
It was pretty good... more than pretty good...

 You wrote a good piece there Melanie...
Can we have a quiet word?
Excuse us for a moment Mr. Brookes won't you?"

DIRECTION

Ms. Jones /Lecturer leads Mel a little way from Mr. Brookes, and the small stage, to the (plays) centre stage.
Mr Brookes goes back sheepishly to his little desk, looking a tad disappointed. He busies himself once more with his paperwork>

DIALOGUE

Ms. JONES/LECTURER

"I just wanted to let you know that I was really impressed Mel.

I would be very happy to incorporate that work into your independent project if you want to submit it.

Any- how think on it, but I would formally advise you, that it would enhance your marks without a doubt.
We can confirm your decision tomorrow.

I think it would also be beneficial to you, as that would lessen your workload if you use it.
But either way there is no problem with your final mark up to now.

Just keep on going as you are.

Well I'm off now.
Well done, it was good fun. Enjoy the rest of your night."

DIRECTION

Mel nods but she just seems rooted to the spot. Lost in her thoughts.

Ms. JONES turns to go, walks away a little then turns back around looking at Mel. She has second thoughts. She picks up on Mel's loneliness. She places her hand onto Mel's elbow.

DIALOGUE

MS. JONES/ LECTURER

" It was good you know Mel, very good.

 But even more than that; it was nice to see you smiling and out with your friends.
It's not all about work you know; this is not the real world...

Though important; this is just a course.
It is just a chapter Mel, however important it is, it is just a chapter.

There is life outside of these three years!
Remember that Mel.. it will be over and you will have the real world to contend with and navigate ..
 A good life and friends is what really matters...being happy when you can.

Anyhow you'll be ok.
See you soon.

As I said .Have a good night !"

DIRECTION

Ms Jones leaves...
Mr Downes sees she is going and scrambles after her.
Jenni and Josh have moved over to Mr Brookes.
They whisper in his ear:

Mel stands a lonely figure. Not certain what to do next.
Like a fish out of water she looks a solitary individual.

A Spotlight comes onto Mel as the scene around her darkens.

A disembodied voice calls out from the stage.

It is the chap Mr. Brookes who was previously manning the table by the stage. The 'MC' for the evening.

He is now back on the stage speaking into the Microphone.

DIALOGUE

MC/ Mr. BROOKES

" Yeah, that was all pretty good...

I've been told by Jen & Josh here that Mel has another good number that we could end the night on..

So Mel, if we could persuade you to come on up again?
We're ready for you.."

DIRECTION

JOSH & JENNI (Start up a chant:)

"MEL-AN-IE, MEL-AN-IE."

It catches on around the room, and soon most of the room are joining in, and clapping to the chants beat.

Not knowing what to do, what else she could possibly do, Mel walks slowly towards the stage. She begins to speak eventually.

DIALOGUE

MELANIE (Said to Mr Brookes)

" Look I don't have any other twenties or relevant songs prepared. I don't know what to sing"

MR BROOKES (Said whilst bending down to talk quietly to Mel from the stage)

" It doesn't have to be 20's or relevant number now Mel. You've done that part.

This really is just for fun. Nothing else."

MELANIE (Said to no one in particular, other than herself?)

"There's that word again. Why don't they all get that I don't do fun? That I don't know how. For real."

JENNI

" Just sing what you feel Mel...just sing what you feel to sing"

JOSH

" You know the right thing to do Mel! You always know the right thing to do..."

DIRECTIONS

Melanie finally gets up onto the stage.
Mel walks over to the tech guys, she takes some music out from her bag gives it to the tech guys has a quick chat with them, then walks back to the microphone centre stage. She throws her bag down, as before.

Mel braces herself and holds fast to the microphone.
Finally she sings out:

'SETTING THE STANDARD' (FULL VOCAL VERSION)

The bar slowly quietens down, as if in response to the sincerity of the music.

As if the lyrics were too poignant to bear.

Some people are slightly swaying to the music.

When the song is over people come up to Mel to say:

PASSERS BY

DIALOGUE

" That was lovely Mel. Really lovely
" How come you're not a star girl? How come?"

DIRECTION

Mel answers sadly:

MELANIE

" I think it's because I don't know how to have fun.
Fuh true"

End of Scene Twenty

<u>Scene Twenty- One Begins</u>

<u>SETTING Beautiful Garden South Of France.</u>
<u>HOT DAY.</u>
<u>At Bella's Farmhouse</u>

<u>DIRECTIONS</u>

Mel is found in a beautiful garden.
She is swaying in a hammock.
It is a hot day in a place far away from London.
Mel is humming a tune to herself <u>('Chained in My Mind')</u>

From across the garden a woman appears with a tray of cooling drinks complete with iced jug.

This is Bella. (The owner of the property.)
Bella is white, attractive and very composed.

Bella places the tray onto a nearby table, and sits down.

She looks about a decade older than Mel.

They are both dressed to stay cool in hot weather.
Bella sits down in a chair at the table.
She calls out to Mel.

<u>DIALOGUE</u>

<u>BELLA</u>

" Thought you might need some cooling down refreshment.
God, I don't know how you can stand this heat out here.
Generally I stay indoors at this time.
 But there again I expect you are used to it"

<u>MEL</u>

"You mean you people, because I'm black,
You think we just meant to be fried to death…"

<u>BELLA</u>

(Replies in a chiding voice)

" No.
 That's not what I meant or think…

I just thought you might be more able to take the heat as you have
travelled so much more than I have…

Nothing to do with being black…
You're too touchy…
Come and have your drink"

DIRECTION

Mel gets up from the hammock and joins Bella at the table.
Bella pours out the drinks for them both.

Mel begins to sip her drink, and starts to apologise to Bella.

MELANIE

"Mmm This is lovely..

I'm sorry Bella, I just… I'm just a bit tetchy.
I'm not sure why.. nor what's wrong with me..
Thinking too much I guess.

Look. Thanks for taking me in.
I love it here..
And I _am_ grateful you know..
For your friendship and everything.

After this break, I'll be able to get myself sorted out properly when I get
back to London.

I'm sure when I can get to speak to Daddy he will let me come home.
If only for a while; until I get myself sorted out.
So, then I will be out of your hair soon, and you then can have some
peace at last."

BELLA

" You don't have to thank me Mel, nor do you have to hurry back.
Just take your time, and enjoy the rest.

We all love having you around..
That's what this place is for.. R & R
Rest and recuperation and rock & roll!"

DIRECTION

Mel and Bella laugh out loud together.

Both women then go quiet with their own thoughts.
They start to toy with their drinks..

At one point Bella holds her drink to her forehead....
And sighs with the heat.
She is still wilting from the heat of the Day.

Mel continues:

MELANIE

"I don't know Bella.

It's all so silly and difficult.
She just never let's me speak to him.

 Whenever I ring she answers, and she always says he's at work or out
or something.
No one is out all the time.

She's just lying to me...keeping me away from him, and the facts
from him too.

He's no idea of what is going on, or what has been going on.
I'm sure he's not aware, that he is under the illusion that Simon and I
are together still.

I've even written letters; but as yet there's been no word back."

BELLA

284

"Well the post here can be somewhat erratic at times.. but not when it comes to bills!
Funny that!

Maybe something will arrive tomorrow..
Most things do here.. Arrive tomorrow that is!

It's just which tomorrow that is the question! (They both smile a little)

I once had a plumber tell me he was coming around on Thursday..
Which he did.
Eventually..
Only trouble was he hadn't made it clear which Thursday..!

Still as he said, he was true to his word, and he never had said exactly which one...so:
I guess Thursday is Thursday.. No matter which one it is!"

DIRECTIONS

Bella laughs at her own joke..
But then senses Mel's sadness and frailty..

BELLA (Continues:)

"Sorry I'm twittering on..
Must be the heat! Well, no, not really.

I do it whatever the weather.

Sometimes, when I'm not sure what to say to comfort or maybe what solution to propose. I just talk.
I have to watch that.. this feeling compelled to help.
Even when I know I can't, I look for solutions...
When really it's not my place to"

DIRECTION

Bella puts her hand on top of Mel's.

"Look Mel, all I should say is, I'm sure it will all get sorted out when you go back. One way or another.

But, it's you who have the answers. No one else.

As for your Mother, she's maybe just angry with you.
Not that she should be..

But people react to things differently..
Her anger will pass, when she realises it's your life, Not hers."

MELANIE (Spoken quietly)

" All she ever says is that marriage is for life and that I should find
Simon and go back to how things were.

That I'll never get any one like him again.

By that she means a good white man...
That's all she really cares about."

DIRECTION/DIALOGUE

MELANIE (Said whilst staring into space).

"But maybe I don't want..." (BIG PAUSE and sigh)

MELANIE (Continues:)

"She's always been the same.
She doesn't care about Simon or me.

She's no idea what we have been through.
Both of us.
All she's bothered about is what her friends in Church and all that will
think or will say....So she's hiding the facts from everyone.
They all will think we still together too."

DIRECTION

Mel holds her glass up high looking through it to the sky. As if
looking for inspiration:

MELANIE

"You can never go back Bella.
Never.
What is done is done, and what is lost has gone forever."

DIRECTION

Bella places her arm on Mel's shoulder to try to comfort her, even more.

BELLA

" You'll be fine Mel. Just enjoy this break...
Recharge and later you will see things clearer.

She will relent.
She is your Mother after all: and she loves you.
She maybe just can't see things the way you do.. and vice versa.
She can't help it.
You'll see.."

DIRECTION

Mel begins to laugh.
She looks around...

DIALOGUE

MELANIE

" You've never met Moira have you?
That's why you can say that."

DIRECTION

Mel sips from her glass.
She sits back in her chair and stretches out...

MELANIE (Continues:)

"I really do love it here Bella..
It reminds me of Trinidad... when I was very teeny..

I could stay in this garden forever.

I know why you love it so.

But it's not a real option.

It would be like passing up on life before I have had one!

Do you know what I think Bella?

If that's what love produces: I don't want any more of it in my life..
Not now not ever"

BELLA (Looks into Mel's eyes with a sad gaze.)

" I am so sorry you feel that way Mel.. I hope those feelings will pass.

Everything changes.. Nothing stays the same..

She must have some feelings for you, surely she can't be all bad?"

MELANIE

" That's what I used to think Bella, what I used to hope..
But I've done with false hopes and dreams.
All she ever taught me in the end was to be quiet, repress things, not
talk .....

Just accept.
Be subservient. Be scared.
I guess that's why I still have so much to learn..

I missed out so much in growing up.. Not knowing how to be with
people; how to mix, to lime.

I guess that's why I am so shy
Repressed even..

Oh, I don't know Bella. I just genuinely don't know what to do now.

I feel I have lost everything before I had anything to lose.
It's a very strange feeling, that I can't put into words."

DIRECTION

Mel suddenly sits up erect and positive.

DIALOGUE

MELANIE (Continues:)

"Well I have to be done with that now!

I'm just scared of how long it will take me to unlearn all that poisonous stuff that was put into me.

How long Bella?"

DIRECTION

Both women sip their drinks whilst staring at the beauty of their surroundings.
Bella sits up straight in excitement.

BELLA

"I can't tell you that Mel.
I'm still working on that one myself.

All I can say is, it does get easier.. But never gets easy.
And that's the truth.

But Mel, don't forget the good stuff that was given to you from those who loved you

Let the love win out Mel,
Let the love melt all that other stuff away."

DIRECTION

Bella charges her glass in a toast, and Mel charges her glass back.
The women smile at one another, and laugh.

BELLA (Continues)

"Look: Let's make a pact, to begin the new life tonight for sure or is that for true?

Whatever.

You know we're having some company tonight...
We might even take in the local fete.. fireworks and all..

We can celebrate new beginnings for all of us.
Especially you!
So, stay here and rest up...
Then you'll be the life and soul tonight.

We'll enjoy some new faces, eh?

Whilst it is good for you to have time to think alone.
It's even better to have time to mix and laugh too."

DIRECTION

With that Bella gets up and heads back to the house taking the tray back with her, leaving the jug of drink and her glass with Mel.

Bella turns back a little to speak to Mel again.
Bella's voice changes to a most serious tone..

DIALOGUE

BELLA

"Don't stay chained to the past Mel: whatever you do.
A lot of time can be lost that way.. and life is too precious to waste..
I should know."

MELANIE

"O.K Bella... I'll try really hard not to.
Thanks Bella.. Thanks for everything.

I do feel a little tired so I will rest up a tad longer as you said.

I will try to let things go.. I really will try. See you later"

DIRECTIONS

With that Bella disappears from view into the house to prepare for the evenings revelry.

Mel continues to sit in her chair, she then gets up and starts to wander about the garden..
She begins to pick some flowers, making a daisy chain.
She then sings:

'CHAINED IN MY MIND' (FULL VOCAL VERSION)

At the end of the song:
A ghostly image of Simon appears at the bottom of the garden..
He is waving and mouthing his final goodbye.

SIMON

" Go out and Find happiness Mel!
Goodbye fuh true..."

Scene Twenty – One Ends

Scene Twenty – Two Begins

SETTING

Inside the kitchen of Bella's old farmhouse.

Outside: Fireworks can be heard from the local fete.
Together with noise from partygoers in Bella's house and garden

Later that day. Early evening:

Opens onto Bella's kitchen.
Mel is talking on the 'phone to her Mother/ Moira.
Bella is in another room off, banging about a bit, getting things ready
for the evening.

There are party noises off.

A familiar conversation is going on.
We can now hear only Mel's voice:

DIALOGUE

MELANIE

" Mummy, please allow me to have my say…"

(Space)

"No, I can't go back"

(Space)

"Why?
Because there is no back to go to."

(Bigger Space)

"Mummy, we can't do it… it all hurts too much."

(Pause)

"Please let me come home. let's start again..
We could be the best of friends..."

(Pause)

<u>**DIRECTIONS**</u>

<u>**'EVERY DAY IS LIKE AN OPERA'**</u>

Partial Vocal in the background

"Please allow me to have my say
We could be the best of friends >>"

<u>**DIALOGUE**</u> (Continues:)

<u>**MELANIE**</u>

" Why won't you let me speak to Daddy?
I know he would help me..
He would let me come home..
If only for a while.. So I can start up again.

He would never turn his back on me"

(Space)

" But Mummy I have nowhere <u>to</u> go."

(Space)

" No. I can't stay here.. This is just for a holiday...
Mummy please..."

<u>**DIRECTION**</u>

<u>**CLICK.**</u> The 'phone goes dead. Moira has hung up on Mel.

<u>**TOTAL SILENCE**</u>

Mel stands for a while with the telephone dangling from her hand.

Mel then calls out to Bella over the melee, which can now be heard again from off stage: Mel lies to Bella:

<u>DIALOGUE</u>

<u>MELANIE</u> (Feigning excitement)

"Bella..!
Bella!
I'm going home..

You were right. Mummy changed her mind.. "

<u>DIRECTIONS</u>

Bella comes bustling into the room carrying a vase of flowers.
She walks across to Mel.
She is beaming:

Mel is crying, but she continues to speak:

<u>MELANIE</u>

" Everything's all right now. I can go home.
Just as you said it would be.

I'll get fixed up with a job and things will be just fine.
Everything's going to be just fine"

<u>BELLA</u>

"Heh Mel that's great!
Fine AND dandy;
Fine and Dandy.

See, I told you the old witch would come around.
These things just take time.."

<u>DIRECTIONS</u>

Bella stops in her tracks, as she becomes aware that Mel is crying..
Bella places the vase of flowers onto a side table.

She reaches out to Mel.

<u>BELLA</u>

" So what's all this then?
Why are you crying so?"

<u>MELANIE</u>

" Oh I guess it's just the relief.

She wants me to leave, to go home tomorrow. Typical eh?

One minute she says never to darken her door again stuff.
The next it's get here fast!

I never could understand that woman.

Anyhow; I had better go sooner rather than later before she changes her
mind; eh?"

<u>DIRECTIONS</u>

They both smile in agreement..
Bella looks at Mel curiously.

They hug.

<u>BELLA</u>

"Well that's true.. You never know.

But I will miss you so... we all will.
Are you sure you are O.K?"

<u>DIRECTION</u>

Melanie nods and wipes her tears with her hand..
Bella reaches out to a box of tissues and hands them to Mel.
Mel takes one and blows her nose.

<u>BELLA</u> (Continues:)

"You do know you now owe me several boxes of tissues!
Which you will have to replace next time you come.

(They hug again and giggle.)

Still it's a pity you can't stick around a little while longer...
There's so much partying to be had yet this summer!

Next time eh?

I thought you were just beginning to get the hang of this mixing and
holiday thing...
And, more to the point you were beginning to look rested, and even
getting over that hospital stuff"

DIRECTION

BELLA (Smiles and hugs Mel again. Bella Continues:)

"But there I go again! This is good news.. it is what you wanted..

You know what they say, when it feels right, then it probably is right.

I'm sure you will feel a whole lot less stressed when you are safely back
home, putting your plans into place at last.

That new start Mel, that new start is about to happen."

MELANIE

"I know, it's a bit scary. What's that saying Bella?
Be careful what you wish for, because you just might get it!

Thanks for everything Bella..
I don't know what I would have done without you"

BELLA

" Give over!
All I know is I'm so pleased for you Mel.
You can now start over with your life.

Put all that stuff behind you.
Remember to let it go Mel...
No more chains Mel; Let it all go.
Somehow."

DIRECTION

Bella takes Mel's hand gently pulling her towards the other room and garden off to where the party's action is happening:

BELLA

"So Mel, let's enjoy tonight's bacchanal as you would say!

AND as you also always say:

Your 'free papers burning fast' girl, it's burning fast!
So, there's no time to lose"

MELANIE

"There's no more sitting on the side lines for me from now on either Bella eh?"

DIRECTION

With that, both Mel and Bella run off to join the Party.

A wild rendition of 'DESIRE' (PARTIAL Version) from (c.d. player) Is now clearly heard from the party in another room and from the garden

This is followed by 'DESIRE' FULL VOCAL VERSION)
(From c.d. Player)

Another Set Dance party scene is re enacted >
Very similar to the Opening Trinidad Party scene.

Only this time Melanie is seen to and gets to, join in fully.

Scene Twenty-Two Ends

<u>Scene Twenty- Three Begins</u>

<u>Setting: Back in London.</u>
<u>Dark wet street scene.</u>
<u>Mel is walking along wearing a coat and carrying a hold all and two
plastic bags.</u>

<u>DIRECTIONS</u>

Mel is knocking on a door.. It is very late.
Mel is dishevelled, very wet and shivering a little.

The door opens.
Jenni pops her head around the door cautiously and is shocked to see
Mel standing on her doorstep.

<u>DIALOGUE</u>

<u>JENNI</u>

" Oh my God.. Mel!
What you doing here?
I thought you was away somewhere.

Thought you were in some high flying job or something what with
you're First an all...

What you doing slumming it here then? "

<u>DIRECTION</u>

Melanie appears to be not only straggly but also ill and exhausted.
She is literally dripping wet.

Mel almost falls into the doorway, and consequently into the hallway.

<u>DIALOGUE</u> (continues)

<u>JENNI</u>

"Well I guess you in now girl!
Heh, are you alright?"

DIRECTION

Jenni now realises that something is wrong.
Her voice softens to one of concern.

Mel starts to cough and has all but collapsed into the hallway.
Jenni puts her arm out to steady Mel.

She calls out into the flat.

Setting Inside Hall
Then later in Sitting Room of small run down London Flat.
Josh & Jenni's Home.

JENNI

"Josh! come out here!"
We need a hand.

Heh Josh, you'll never guess what the rain blew in!
Literally"

DIRECTION

Though Jenni was reluctant at first to open up to Mel,
She can now see Mel is looking ill.

Jen offers her arm for Mel to lean on.
Jenni's tone becomes even more one of concern.

MELANIE

" I'm sorry to barge in like this Jen.
But, I couldn't think of any one else who would help me out.

It's only for tonight, until I get myself sorted out.

I can sleep on the floor.. it's just for tonight, Jen..
Just for tonight"

JENNI

" God Mel what happened to you?"

DIRECTION

After sounds of much kerfuffle, Josh arrives on the scene.
He quickly takes the plastic bags and then the hold all from Mel.

Josh appears shocked and concerned as Mel begins to cough.

DIALOGUE

JOSH

"Oh my God Mel! What's happened to you..? You look awful"

JENNI

"Nice one Josh just what a girl wants to hear!

Anyhow, shut up Josh we already did that one!
Let's get her inside properly."

DIRECTION

Jenni turns her attention back fully to Mel as she helps Mel inside the flat.
They all bundle into the sitting room, with Josh doing his best to juggle with Mel's various bags.

JENNI (Continues)

"Come on Mel.
What you need is a hot drink inside you, and to take off that wet coat.."

DIRECTION

Jen turns to Josh.

JENNI

"Josh, put Mel's stuff over there and then go and make some tea..."

DIRECTIONS

Josh places the bags down on the floor at the side of the sofa.
He then does as he is told, and scurries into the kitchen.
(Kitchen noises are later heard off.)

Meanwhile, Jenni has guided Mel over to a comfy solitary sofa.
Jenni begins to take Mel's wet coat off her, and throws it over the back
of the sofa.

Once the coat is removed Mel sits/ plonks herself down gratefully.
She sinks into the sofa, in a bit of a pile.

Mel stares into space silently.
Jenni sits on the floor at Mel's feet.

There is a long pause.
Maybe both are not sure what to say.
They are both taking in the new situation.

Jenni is first to break the silence.
Jenni speaks nervously at first and rather quickly..

(She later calms down.)

JENNI

*"Look Mel there's something you should know.
I mean Josh and me, we kinda got together, proper like.
As you may have gathered.
We always got along good and that.*

*I hope you don't mind?
After Uni, well we kinda of stuck around and you know how tings go!
And I've always liked him.
Well you know, he clueless, but he kind of cute with it...."*

DIRECTIONS

This makes Mel giggle softly....a little.

301

Mel now comes back to the now, to focus on Jenni.

MELANIE

"Mind, Jen?
Why should I mind?

It's great. It's wonderful.
My two best friends together... What could be better?

You two belong together..
I mean who else would you tell what to do and to shut up if not Josh eh?"

DIRECTIONS

They both laugh a bit sheepishly...Mel still coughs a little too.
Jenni calls through to Josh.

DIALOGUE

JENNI

" Heh Josh, get a move on.
And can you get a dry towel from the bathroom while you are at it?"

MELANIE

" See what I mean?
Made for one another"   (Said shaking her head)

DIRECTIONS

The two women hug.. and smile.
(Jenni has become wet from hugging Mel. She shakes herself dry)

JENNI

"You need to dry off badly girl eh?"

(Slight Pause)

<u>JENNI</u> (Continues:)

"Oh Mel, come to think of it, it is <u>good</u> to see you...
But not like this.
What has been going on? What's happened to you?
To be true, girl, I cannot lie to you, you do look kinda of rough.
Not the Mel of old!"

MELANIE

" To tell <u>you</u> the truth Jen I'm not sure, how I got to this point.
Maybe I became a tad numb.
Just drifted into being a bit lost, and then a bit broke, then a bit
homeless!   (Mel gives an ironic laugh)

That's about all I can tell you. I guess it can happen to anyone if they
take their eye off the ball.   (Mel gives another weak smile)

But, it is just temporary, it just for now. I'll sort it all out.
The difference is I'm now ready, to sort it all out"

JENNI

"I can't believe this!
I mean we hadn't heard from you since the end, you know since
graduation and that.
And with us not exactly getting a degree at all, never mind a first we
figured you had dumped us.

You know, gone off to bigger and better things...
Not scrunting like us in some measly dump like this"

DIRECTION

At this, Josh walks in from the kitchen carrying three teas on a rusty
old tray. He puts them down onto a small coffee table.

JOSH

"Heh I heard that!

Mind what you say about my measly dump, any place is better than
no place at all.
In bloody London you're lucky to get <u>anything</u> at all!

Ain't that so Mel? Oh sorry, I didn't mean to, what I mean is, well...
So, How's the two old guards, Mum and Dad then Mel?
So what's the story?"

<u>MELANIE</u>

"There's no big story really Josh.
Just a run of the mill thing...
I just find myself alone.. with no one to turn to and with no where to
go to. Except here, to beg a bed for the night.

I'm so sorry to bug you all."

<u>JOSH</u>

" But I thought your folks and your sister were close by, here in
London. What happened there?"

<u>MELANIE</u>

" You remember that guy who came to see me when we were in halls?"

<u>JENNI</u>

" Yeah we remember him. Don't we Josh? I know he was...
Well, eventually even Cluedoh Josh here managed to kind of work it
out"

<u>MELANIE</u> (Interrupts)

" Yes.
Well you guessed right Josh.

At the time I just couldn't talk about it properly, not even to Jen here.
Just skirted around it.

I told her not to mention to you..

304

I didn't know how to. Talk. Not talk things out properly.
It just didn't happen in my family. At all.

I wasn't meaning to hide things from you all…
I just didn't know <u>how</u> to talk things out.

I'm a bit better at sharing stuff now though."

DIRECTION

Josh hands Mel her tea.
She pauses then sips some, and shivers a little. Again she coughs.

MELANIE (Continues:)

"We were married, and now we're not …for good.

And my Mother well, she doesn't understand …
In her world you stay together whatever…
And I mean whatever!

It's no-one's fault, it's just the way it is…

But she; well I guess you could say she has turned her back on me.
Maybe she thinks that will make us get back together…

But it's not like that… things don't work like that.
Only in her world.
She has her beliefs..

The world has moved on…but she has stayed stuck to the past.
A place I don't want to ever get stuck in…chained to.

I nearly did… But not now!

Well, now I want to live in this century."

JOSH

" Good for you Mel!
You always were feisty!

So.
What does your old Dad say to all of this?"

MELANIE

" I have no idea really, I never get to talk with him ..

She keeps him away from any contact with me..
Even my letters are never answered..
I suppose she's told him a load of lies.
Who knows.

And you know what Josh, at this point I _truly_ don't care any more."

JENNI

" Come on Mel have some more tea... it'll warm you up a bit.
Josh did you get that Towel?   (Said whilst turning on Josh)

Mel's still dripping and shivering!
Let's get her dried out properly!"

JOSH

"OK keep your nickers on. I'm on to it!"

DIRECTION

Josh scoots off to the bathroom and returns with a towel.
Mel sips more tea.
She is beginning to thaw out a little.

Josh hands the towel to Mel.
She begins to rub down her face and hair.

Mel hands the wet towel back to Josh.
Josh throws the towel onto a small chair.

Mel then sips her tea again.

Josh and Jenni exchange looks of bewilderment, and concern.

DIALOGUE

MELANIE

"Gosh that's better. Thanks.

I didn't realise how cold I was...

I must look like a wreck!"

JENNI

" Well as I said, I can't lie to you, it's not your finest moment!"

DIRECTION

Melanie smiles and wraps her hands around her tea for warmth.
She shivers again.

DIALOGUE.

MELANIE

"It's true what they say there is nothing like a good cup of tea"

JOSH

" Why do I think the next line is, and this is nothing like..."

DIRECTION

With that the ice is truly broken.
All three laugh at the weak joke.

MELANIE

"It's just.
It's just; I just want the chance to start my life again my way...

I've let that woman control my life for so long.
Enough is enough.

It's been my whole life up to now..
And now it stops. Right now.

I'm taking control, whatever it takes, I'm taking control"

DIRECTION

Everyone goes silent, not knowing what to say. Josh nods.
Mel gazes into space. Josh and Jenni just stare at one another.

Mel sips more tea and sighs a tired relieved sigh.

She pops her teacup back onto the coffee table,
and lies back gratefully, sinking into the sofa.

MELANIE

"I've come a long way and I just need..
I just need to rest.. I'll be gone by morning Jen.

I just need one night and I will sort something out tomorrow.
In the morning"

JENNI

" We only have this sofa to offer you Mel.
But you know you can stay as long as it takes, don't you?
There's no hurry. Isn't that so Josh?
We just have the one bed and that's a single.
But we'll all manage eh!"

DIRECTION

Josh now sits next to Mel on the sofa and puts his arms around her.

JOSH

"As long as it takes Mel.. No problemo.
We're more than glad to be of assistance to My Lady Mel!"

JENNI

"Josh! go hang Mel's coat up.

Please...

And while you're at it, take that wet towel back into the bathroom"

DIRECTION

Jenni looks at Mel's wet coat.
Josh gets up from the sofa.

Josh picks up Mel's wet coat, then the wet towel.
He shuttles off with Mel's wet coat to the hall.

JOSH

"Anything else whilst I'm at it my Supremo?"

DIALOGUE

JENNI

"As it happens, yeah. Sort out some bedding for Mel here!"

(Jenni turns her attention back to Mel, whilst Josh can be heard going into the bathroom with the wet towel, and later into the bedroom.)

JENNI (Continues)

"Look Mel, I'm sorry about the welcome! Or lack of it.
We really did think you had gone off us.
You don't have to explain anything to us really.
All you need to know is that you welcome here.
You're _our_ friend.
And that's that.
So, just get your rest, and don't worry so. Things will work out.
They usually do one way or another.

I'll go and get the bedding ..
A blanket or something..
Cluedoh will never find it"

DIRECTION

Jenni gets up to go to the bedroom to get the bedding herself.
She calls out to Mel

JENNI

"Oih Mel! You hungry, or what?
We can manage a boiled egg or something.
I'm not sure if we can offer you a shower...
Slight problemo with the old leccy card..

But don't worry we can sort something out tomorrow eh
We good at that. We've had plenty of practice. Sorting out tomorrows."

DIRECTION

Josh returns, as Jenni is making her way to the bedroom.
They almost bump into one another.
Josh whispers into Jenni's ear.

JENNI

"Oh, it seems we don't have any food to speak of."
(Said to Mel, as if it is Josh's fault)

DIALOGUE

JOSH

" I can go out and get some.. Only.   (Said in an embarrassed tone)

Jen. Do you have any cash on you? I'm a bit short."
(Half whispered to Jen)

JENNI (Half whispered back. Impatiently.)

" God Josh you are always broke... !"

DIRECTION

Jen picks up her bag from the floor.

310

(Jenni & Josh are obviously struggling financially.)

JENNI

"Here I have a few bob in my bag.
(Jen thrusts some money into Josh's hand.)

I'll just go and get that blanket and stuff for Mel"

MELANIE

" Don't worry Jen. I'm ok for now.
I think I am too tired to eat...or shower or anything else come to that.

Maybe tomorrow...
We'll _all_ sort ourselves out then eh?"

DIRECTIONS

Jenni leaves to go to the bedroom.

Josh goes back to sitting next to Mel on the sofa.

DIALOGUE

JOSH

" I'm really sorry for your troubles Mel... it must be tough when your
folks do that.. I don't get it..
I mean, you would think we were in the last century!

But where have you been meanwhile for all this time?"

MELANIE

" Oh I met someone ...

Someone who was, who was kind to me.
I stayed at their place in France for a while...

Just to sort my head out a little.
Just liming really.

You know what it's like when you finish Uni…
It can be a bit disorientating, until you find your way again…

It's a bit like 'so what now!'

All the deadlines have been met…and you are left alone, with…
There is just a big vast empty calendar.

But, Now I'm back…. In the real world.

It was only a course, not the real world eh?
I'm going to have to fill those dates up somehow…
Make a life.

And make a living!"

JOSH

" I guess you're right.
But we did have some fun didn't we?"

MELANIE (Said whilst placing her hand onto Josh's arm in a soft moment)

" We did Josh. And we made some fine memories too."

DIRECTIONS

Jenni returns in a bustle, with a sheet, pillow and a meagre cover.

MELANIE (Continues:)

" I was just saying to Josh, how we did make some fine memories, when we were at Uni!"

JENNI (Said almost overlapping one another)

" Heh Mel! This is the best we can muster up…but it should keep you warm enough.   (Pause. Sigh)

"Yes.. I guess we did…"   (Smile)

312

DIRECTIONS

The two women stop and look at one another intently.
Jenni places the bedding next to Mel on to the sofa.

DIALOGUE

JENNI

" There you go Mel.
I, _we_ really do mean it Mel, you can stay as long as you need to.
You are our best friend fuh true!

Anyhow, I know you'll soon get sorted out... won't she Josh?"

JOSH

"Of Course she will.
But Please! Stay as long as you can bear to!
It'll be fun...Like the old days, the three of us together.

Anyhow, the oldies will come 'round, soon enough.
Parents always do.

Especially when you get that big shot job.
That'll move them into action.
(Said turning to Jenni)

Mel was just telling me where's she's been all this time...
Weren't you Mel? You'll never guess!"

MELANIE

" Oh yes ...   (Mel tails off a little sleepy; then revives.)

I was in France for a while...just brakesing 'till I could get sorted,
you know.
Someone was kind to me, offered me a break.

But I knew I had to get back...
That all I was doing was avoiding reality.
Now I am back to face up to it all.

I want to be on the rise again... I'm sooo tired of being down.
I want to be on the rise again.. Take control..."

DIRECTIONS

At this point Mel appears to be flagging.. almost asleep..
Mel's head has fully rested onto the back of the sofa.
JENNI (Said softly to Josh, whilst pulling him up from the sofa.)

"Ssh...Come on Josh.
Let's get our teas in us.. Then get some shut eye"

MELANIE   (Only half awake)

"Thanks you two.. You've saved my life fuh true"

JENNI

" Rubbish... a cup of tea and a sofa ...
How can that save anyone's life?"

MELANIE (Said in a very serious tone)

" Sometimes. That's all it takes!

You opened your door to me when my own wouldn't...
Shown me more love than they ever have.
I will never forget that. Not ever! I love you guys the most!

(Mel yawns)

I think I will go to sleep now if that's alright with you?"

DIRECTIONS

Jenni and Josh both bend down to hug Mel in turn.
They turn around and creep towards the bedroom.
By the time they reach the doorway Mel seems to be fast asleep.

DIALOGUE

JENNI (Softly)

"Night Night Mel"

JOSH (Softly)

" Night Night Mel."

JENNI (Whispered to Josh as they reach the bedroom door)

" How the hell are we going to hide her from the landlord?
You're already hiding me!"

DIRECTIONS

There has been no answer from Mel. It seems she is already fast asleep.

Josh goes back over to Mel and puts the covers over her properly.
He walks back to Jenni.
They kiss.

Jenni turns out the light.

The stage goes black. A voice is heard after Jenni and Josh have left.
It is

MELANIE (Said almost in her sleep)

" I'll be gone by morning, before deh up and all.
I have to rise myself up somehow!
I can't take them down with me eh?
They have troubles enough without me bringing em down no further.
And that is the truth. "

CLOSE of Scene Twenty- Three

BLACK STAGE

<u>Scene Twenty- Four Begins</u>

<u>SETTING</u>
<u>LONDON STREET SCENE</u>. <u>The Next Night.</u>

It is a very sleety cold night.

Mel is seen from the back walking with her hold all and plastic bags.

The MUSIC is playing

Mel turns to sing to the audience:

<u>A HOME THAT'S ALL MINE</u>   (<u>Full CHORAL vocal version</u>)

<u>CLOSE of SCENE Twenty- Four</u>

<u>Scene Twenty- Five Begins</u>

<u>SETTING Melanie's Beautiful Palatial Sitting Room.</u>
<u>It is filled with many Flowers and Plants.</u>

<u>Some years later.</u>

Mel is sitting at a piano... she is composing a tune.
She is alone.

Prominently displayed above the Piano are three framed photographs.
One is of Mel. One is of Grandma.
And is one EMPTY.

Mel is singing/ humming quietly to herself, along to a Very Partial
Piano instrumental of <u>'Someone Out There.'</u>

Mel is interrupted by the 'phone ringing.

She leaves the piano to answer the telephone, which is placed on her desk
over by the window.

<u>DIALOGUE</u>

<u>MELANIE</u>

" Hello, Yes. This is Mel speaking"

(Space)

"OK I'll just get my Diary, please hold on."

<u>DIRECTIONS</u>

Mel puts the 'phone down on the desk for a moment or two.

Mel goes through the pages of her diary, then reaches over to her
computer.

Mel then picks up the 'phone.
She begins to speak again.

<u>DIALOGUE</u>

<u>MELANIE</u>

" Mmm.
It looks as though I could be free around that date.
It sounds like a great gig...

I'll let you know when I've seen the deal, etc"

 (Pause whilst the other person is speaking)

"That seems ok.
I shall email you a number you can call...

They will deal with the details, contract etc.
That is if things go that far."

Mel listens intently.
Mel answers calmly showing no signs of emotion.

(Space)

<u>MELANIE</u> (Continues)

"O.K ... Yes.

 I'll look forward to it.
Thanks. Bye"

Mel puts the 'phone down and gets up from her desk.

Mel stands and gazes out of the window for a long time.

The 'phone rings again.

Mel walks across to answer it.

In a weary voice she says:

<u>DIALOGUE</u>

318

<u>MELANIE</u> (Flatly at first)

" Hello Mel speaking"

(Space)

"Oh, hello Mummy"

(Space)

"I just prefer to use Mel Mummy. (Said in a very weary tone)

Anyhow; what do you want Mummy?
I'm in the middle of something.

In fact I'm in the middle of a lot of things.
I have a very full calendar.."

(Longer Space)

" No, Look Mummy you have to understand, I haven't heard from him in years
Please stop going on as if it were all yesterday..."

(Space)

"Moira! I've told you. Those days are all dead and gone."

(Space)

"I'm sorry. Mummy then. Look, let's change the subject."

(Space)

"How is Daddy? Is he any better?"

(Space)

"Good, that's good... Has he..."

(Moira Interrupts Mel. There is a Long Space)

"No Mummy I'm not seeing anyone…"

(Space)

" Yes, No.
Yes it is very fortunate that Marie gave you a Gran…"

(Space)

"Maybe I'm not normal Mummy.
What is normal Mummy? You I suppose!"

DIRECTION

(Big Space, in which Melanie becomes visibly irritated.)

MELANIE

"Look Mummy, I have to go now, I have to get on."

(Space)

"No Mummy I haven't been to confession..
I've told you many times, I don't even go to church nowadays."

(Even bigger space)

DIRECTION

Mel starts to pace the floor; she is becoming very agitated.
Mel breaks into Mummy / Moira's monologue.

MELANIE

"Look Mummy I <u>have</u> to go; I have a big gig coming up, I have to
prepare, so I <u>really do</u> have to go now."

(Space)

MELANIE

"No Mummy it's not silly. It's what I do nowadays.

Who I am."

(Space)

"No, that time at University wasn't wasted.
I have to go now, Mummy."

(Space)

" Yes I'll think about it..
Yes, I know you're getting older Mummy.."

(Space)

"Yes, Mummy I know... you supposed to love your parents and take
care of them in their old age.."

(Space)

"Yes, Mummy. Yes I do."

(Long Space)

"I know you alone. Yes. No.
Yes Mummy, I do know how it feels. Fuh true.
But yuh no poor-me-one. Yuh have Daddy!"

(Small Space)

"Look Mummy there's someone at the door.
I really _really_ do have to go now.
Yes I will. OK. Bye."

(Another last space!)

"Yes Mummy.   (Said <u>VERY</u> wearily, with sighs.)
I will call you tomorrow.   (Pause)   Yes, I promise"

DIRECTION

Mel puts the 'phone down firmly and walks wearily back to the piano.

321

Mel sighs.
Mel stares and stares at the music, and then up towards the empty photo frame.

DIALOGUE

MELANIE

" Oh poor young Simon .Oh poor young Mel.
"What was done to us, to make such hell?"

MELANIE SUSPENSION/ TURNING TO THE AUDIENCE

" I was always betwixt and between yuh know.

Not really Trini
Not really English..

Not really Grandmas'
Not ever Mummy's

Not Simons ideal even?
I gave him Tabago love...I didn't know how to do any other way
Hiding all meh feelings fuh true!

And now?
Am I Mels' ideal girl? Eh! Me MEH own DNA?

Mummy she did always cuss and fatigue meh.
Always the cut eye at me.

So I never learnt self-confidence.. How to big up
Never was _at ease_ with people.

Not here
Not there
Not anywhere.

She always telling meh I do idiotic.
Keeping me away from carnaval and such. Isolated. Denigrated.

An all kinds of ting like dat!   (Said in Mel's best Trini dialect)

Stopping me from the very way we Trinis' 'speech off' (Trini Dialect)
So's I can be some English Lady and such stuff like dat..

Better myself eh e! Deny my true heritage more like>

<u>Lose myself more like.</u>   (Said in an English accent)

She never 'give me ah chance tuh talk yuh know' (Trini Dialect)
She always turn her back to me

She does kill me yuh know.

Meh have nutten more tuh say."   (All Trini Dialect)

<u>DIRECTION</u>

Melanie turns to the piano to play:

<u>MELANIE</u> (Mel hesitates)

" Except:

So here meh too sit alone
Connected to the world by 'phone.
Me weary of it all fuh true!

English through and through?

So tell me fast or tell me slow!
What it is I supposed to do?"

"Eh e!"

<u>DIRECTION</u>

Melanie starts to play the piano, and sings:

<u>SOMEONE OUT THERE</u>   (FULL Vocal Version)

<u>Scene Twenty- Five Ends Black OUT></u>

<u>Scene Twenty- Six Begins</u>

<u>Setting: Lovely Old THEATRE. Melanie's GIG</u>

<u>DIRECTIONS</u>

Melanie is on stage...with a band.
She is saying thank you to the audience. Throughout, at appropriate moments, the stage gradually becomes peppered with people from her past as the songs progress.

<u>DIALOGUE</u>

<u>MELANIE</u>

" I know it sounds trite but I do want to thank you all for coming tonight. It really does mean so much to me...

My songs are me... Melanie who likes to be called Mel.

My hopes my dreams and my desires are all in the melting pot that is me...My songs.
And possibly therein lies my Destiny Exposed for all to see.

That is my songs.

My Diversity Exposed for all to see and to figure out for yourselves, and me:
My Dreams, my Desires and ultimately my Destiny?"

<u>DIRECTION</u>

<u>MEL</u> (Laughs and continues:)

<u>DIALOGUE</u>

"These last two songs are much more about my future.
At least I hope they are!

Well maybe with a little tinge of my past running through their core.

Please enjoy and stay with Me.. Please stay with me. I implore"

DIRECTION

Mel turns and nods to the band, to begin.

MELANIE

"I look to you all for my Destiny.
But as they say; Man Plans and God?

Well he just laughs.
Doh Make Joke! Fuh True! "

The Music Strikes up and there begins the first of two songs sung as if at a concert. Mel sings:

<u>On The Rise Again</u>   (Full Vocal Version)

Followed by

<u>My Destiny Is Calling</u>   (Full Vocal Version)

DIRECTIONS

On set are dancers dancing.
During the last song in they evoke a party atmosphere.

Mel takes the applause waving and thanking as she begins to leave the stage. She hesitates and looks to her side.

As Mel looks all around the stage (when possible up to the boxes) all the old faces are waving to her ..

They are like ghosts from her past, surrounding her.

Simon is at the Fore Front smiling..

SIMON

" It just wasn't meant to be Mel..
I'm so sorry.."

Mummy & Daddy are there. Somewhat stony faced..

325

MUMMY

" Melanie what you doin out there?
You still making a show of yourself I see fuh true!
Come here! You take care of me, like I did you. I all alone now.
Its yuh duty yuh know. Me poor-me-one for sure now.
He no use to meh now. I lonely.................."

DADDY

" I was wrong Mel , I did wrong..

And I should have stood up to her"
(Said whilst nodding his head toward Moira)

BELLA

" I knew you would do good Mel, don't listen to them.
Put it all behind you... Remember No chains. No chains.

There are other people who love you now"

JOSH

" Heh Girl what's happening? Stay in touch you know.
I'll always have a soft spot for you My Lady Mel"

JENNI

" See Mel it came right in the end eh?
We is We always...innit? Don't worry so!"

CHERIE

" We sisters Mel, We Sisters Forever."

MARIE

" I guess it too late for us now Mel? eh?"

JOANIE, CARRIE & BETSY

SING: A Snippet of: <u>But Aren't You A Jamaican?</u>
Together with <u>A Little dance</u> and (chorus).

Ending with this

<u>DIALOGUE:</u>

" London girls Forever! Yuh cooking' with gas now girl"
(Said whilst waving and blowing kisses to Mel.)

<u>GRANDMA</u> (Looms Large)

" You free now Mel.. You free of them all..
Free to do as you please.
Love as you please and <u>live</u> as you please!"

<u>DIRECTION</u>

Mel wells up a little.

<u>GRANDMA</u> (Continues and blows a kiss to Mel.)

"I hear all the songs Mel
I feel all dem songs Mel

Don't you forget what I tell yuh.
Yuh reconcile now with that Mummy of yours'
Before she go. Life short yuh know. Life too damn short"

Melanie reaches out to Grandma.
But she disappears.

Any other characters can now start to fill up the stage behind:

A FULL Choral Rendition is sung of

<u>**EVERY DAY WAS LKE AN OPERA**</u>

MEL SMILES. Then ALL IS SILENT.

<u>The three 'boys'</u> walk on stage, silently with black hoods over their heads.

<u>My Destiny Is Calling</u>   Is now sung by the full Company with Mel.

NOTE: AS the lyric "My Mama's words>" are sung
Mummy /Moira and Mel hold one another fast and sing together.

<u>Note:</u> MOIRA has a solo part in the song:

"After My Mama's words
Wise up>"

<u>This is a coming together of Mel & Moira at last?</u>

<u>Last DIRECTION</u>

MEL WAVES AND LEAVES THE STAGE TO THE MUSIC:

All Fades into a Black Background with shadows, backed by a Red Sky.

<u>THE END</u>

Of THE PLAY / MUSICAL

END NOTES:

All Characters and the Story line are **Fictional.**
They are not based upon any persons either living at the time of
writing, or dead.

Nothing within this Musical is based upon anything other than the
Songs Used within the Musical, which were all
Written by Wendy Guevara.

And of course this Musical Libretto comes directly from My:
(Elizabeth Gwilliams') Imagination Speciale Only.

Please Note: Any attempts at Trinidadian dialect are done with love,
not enough knowledge: and are open to improvements. **(Sorry)**

The whole of this Libretto is done with love and respect to the characters
within and to all that view it from without.

The reason for writing this Libretto was to highlight and understand
the depth and beauty within Wendy Guevaras' song writing.

It has also been written from a perspective of trying to understand us
all, our relationships and what might contribute to our formation.

Please forgive any mistakes... Fuh True? Doh make Joke!

I am aware that there <u>will</u> be 'mistakes' of one sort or another within
this work. Also that it is (as all work is) open to criticism. Accepted.

I am also aware that as this work goes out into the world, there will be a
need within directors, producers and actors to interpret and bend the
work to their need(s)/interpretation(s).
I appreciate and to some extent accept this as progressive and natural.
It is as I would need and seek to do myself within such roles!

However: I do not want the apple to fall TOO far from the tree, as Moira
would say, without my consent.

After all **this** is the Mothership.

And as such; should be respected, and nurtured.

Therefore; I ask only that, in the future whenever it is reconstituted then reconvened it should also be reconciled to this work.

That always, it should be recognisable, like an old friend who has taken to wearing new clothes, new hair cut, or who is maybe twenty years older than when last seen.

The essence will still be at their core, for all to see.
If only one looks carefully.

For ultimately all comes back to its' origin(s)?

Just like ourselves?

Remember there is a little of us all in all of these fictional characters. The bad, the good and the downright stupidee.

Finally to Wendy Guevara.

This Musical is dedicated to you.

With heartfelt thanks for Your Wonderful Lyrics and for Your Wonderful Music.